7MOMENTS

...THAT DEFINE EXCELLENT LEADERS

LEE J. COLAN

7 Moments

... That Define Excellent Leaders

Inquiries regarding permission for use of the material contained in this book should be addressed to:

> CornerStone Leadership Institute
> P.O. Box 764087
> Dallas, TX 75376
> 888.789.LEAD

Printed in the United States of America
ISBN: 0-9772257-7-1

Credits

Editor	Alice Adams
Proofreader	Elizabeth Young
Design, art direction, and production	Melissa Monogue, Back Porch Creative, info@BackPorchCreative.com

Table of Contents

STARTING THE CLOCK
Defining your moments of Excellence

"There comes a special moment in everyone's life, a moment for which that person was born. That special opportunity, when he seizes it, will fulfill his mission – a mission for which he is uniquely qualified. In that moment, he finds greatness. It is his finest hour."

– Winston Churchill

It was her freshman year at Harvard and the bright-eyed student had just completed her first assignment. The professor collected the papers, and the next day, when the student received her paper back, at the bottom the professor had written, "Is this the best you can do?" The student thought, "No," and redid the paper. It was handed in again and received the same comment. This went on 10 times until finally the student said, "Yes, this is the best I can do." The professor replied, "Fine, now I'll read it."

In college, students are sometimes given second or even third chances to do their best work. However, after graduation, the real world provides very few chances to take our work back for revisions. The challenge and responsibility of leadership offer even fewer second chances.

In today's information-rich and time-poor world, we must build excellence in real time as we juggle competing demands, virtual teams, fluid priorities and high-velocity change. Excellence is not created "when we have time for it." It's built moment by moment.

The building blocks of excellence are moments...literally. That is, defining moments.

According to Nobel Prize winning scientist Daniel Kahneman, we experience thousands of individual moments every waking day. These "moments" last only a few seconds. If you consider your strongest memories, positive or negative, you'll notice the imagery in your mind is actually defined by your recollection of a precise point in time.

In some cases, a single encounter can change your life forever. Think of your own defining moments. Are they literally moments?

Defining moments might be positive or negative, but either way, we are never the same after experiencing one. These moments shape who we are and who we will become. As Mufasa, the Lion King himself, said to his son, Simba, from the heavens, "You are more than you have become." These few words created a positive defining moment for Simba and those around him.

Fantasy or reality, it works the same. So let's look at reality.

We might be defined by a word of encouragement from a colleague or, just as likely, from a word of discouragement. We might be defined by a moment of glorious victory or one of horrendous failure. We might also be defined by a moment of perfect intuition or one where our best judgment was ultimately found faulty. Or perhaps, the moment we commit ourselves to a goal or the moment we decide to go another direction.

We could also be defined by the moment when we decide to make our team's experience different than the ones we had in the past or the moment we experience a positive example and decide to model it for our own team. We may even be defined by the moment a boss lets us know he believes in us or even the moment of honest self-reflection that urges us to take action.

Defining moments, indirectly or directly, create a new direction or perspective for us. Consider runner Georgene Johnson. She got to the starting line of a weekend race 15 minutes early. It was a mistake in timing that became a defining moment in her life.

The 42-year-old secretary had registered to run in a 10 kilometer/ 6.2 mile race that Sunday. The race started at 8:45 a.m. There was also a marathon scheduled to begin 15 minutes earlier. Both races used the same starting line.

Georgene took off at the sound of the starting gun. Four miles down the road, as the race route took the runners out of downtown and into residential areas, Johnson said she experienced a sick feeling that she was possibly in the wrong race. A few minutes later, another runner confirmed her suspicions.

Instead of stopping and retracing her steps, she joined about 4,000 runners taking part in the Revco Cleveland Marathon. Rather than quit, she decided to keep going (no doubt a defining moment!) and hung on to finish her first 26-mile race.

"As stupid as I felt out there running, I'm proud of myself," Johnson said after the race. "I guess I was in better shape than I thought. I feel fine."

Johnson finished the 26-mile marathon in four hours and four minutes, good enough for 83rd place in the women's division – definitely qualifying as one of her life's defining moments. Why? Until that time, her longest run was eight miles.

Like Johnson, we each experience our own defining moments on the road to leadership excellence.

It is important to be aware of our defining moments. They make us who we are. Additionally, **we have the opportunity to create defining moments for our employees** *every day*. In fact, the pathway to leadership excellence is paved with these moments – positive defining moments we create for others.

I remember earlier in my career, I was hungry to advance to an executive leadership position. I thought I was doing all the right stuff, but I wasn't getting there as fast as I had hoped. So I asked a respected friend and colleague what he thought it would take for me to break through to the next level. He sat quietly and thought for a minute, then with penetrating eye contact he slowly advised, "Well, Lee, from my perspective, you should probably focus more on performing your current role excellently than worrying about your next move."

It was incredibly valuable and humbling advice, a defining moment for me and my (never ending) journey toward leadership excellence. This defining moment taught me that excellence is achieved in the moment, not in the future.

This book describes seven moments that define excellent leaders, and each chapter outlines strategies to create defining moments for our teams.

The clock is running. Not a moment to waste. So let's get started!

"If you're doing your very best, you won't have any time to worry about failure."

– H. Jackson Browne

1

A Moment to **COMMIT**

Giving your all-time best

*"Your life changes the moment you make a new,
congruent and committed decision."*

– Anthony Robbins

As we have all learned through some of life's harder lessons – whether it's helping a friend through a tough time, coaching a little league team or working on a critical project – giving our best always gets the best results.

The moment we totally commit ourselves and begin giving 100 percent, a certain momentum develops. People naturally gravitate to those who are committed and start working in the same direction. Total commitment results in a certain, magical boldness – a boldness that has genius and power.

Andrew Carnegie said, "The average person puts only 25 percent of his energy and ability into his work. The world takes off its hat to those who put in more than 50 percent of their capacity and stands on its head for those few and far between souls who devote 100 percent." We compete against our own potential every day.

I personally experienced the power of 100 percent commitment (and lack thereof!) when I wrestled with publishing a book for two years. I was consulting and writing leadership articles, and so I thought it might also be time to write a book. I went through all the motions, from working with agents to sending proposals to writers' conferences, but I never seemed to turn the corner from aspiring writer to published author. There always seemed to be an obstacle, although I now realize it was a result of my less-than-full commitment to my goal.

One obstacle after another...two years and counting. Then one day, I was at a client's office. My defining moment of commitment came when I saw a big box filled with practical handbooks sitting on my client's desk.

I quickly flipped through one of them and jotted down the publisher's name as I said to myself, "I can do this!" My moment of commitment turned into action, and with the incredibly gracious support of the publisher, I had my first book in print six months later. My defining moment helped me envision possibilities that I could only see through fully committed eyes.

Our commitment to our teams can have the same transforming effect. Committed leadership inspires committed teams. During the most challenging time in history for the airline industry, as an example, Southwest Airlines' employees voluntarily forfeited $5 million in vacation time and $1 million in pay to help the company stay financially viable. Employees also took over the lawn and facility maintenance at corporate headquarters. These employees were simply reflecting a deep commitment – personal and professional – they felt from their leadership. When we lead with 100 percent commitment, this is the kind of commitment to excellence we can inspire in return.

Even with 100 percent commitment, however, leadership is not always a smooth flight. If we want to pilot our teams to excellence, we have to understand we can't just kick back in a comfy first-class seat. Now we have responsibility for not only ourselves but also for the success of our teams. Our teams are depending on us to set a good course, keep them posted on our progress and make smart decisions.

Jumping into the pilot's seat brings many more responsibilities than privileges. But those who are defined by their 100 percent commitment to leadership excellence reap the rewards of flying high above the rest!

Here are three strategies to seize your moment to commit:

- Think excellence
- Create a compelling cause
- Secure your foundation.

Think Excellence

Excellent leadership is defined by excellent thinking. Words and acts of excellence are preceded by thoughts of excellence.

Our minds are magnets. What we focus on is what we get. Our thoughts and beliefs have that much power. Think about it! We receive what we believe about leadership. This works just as powerfully with negative thoughts as it does with positive thoughts.

You might be asking, "How can I be positive all the time when negative situations are a reality – they just show up in everyday life?"

Yes, bad things do happen and they sometimes "just show up." Any leader would be hard pressed to remember a week when no curve balls were thrown at him. However, it is our interpretation that makes a situation negative. A surprise event or a challenging moment doesn't drag us down. The way we think about what happens determines the ultimate outcome.

Like it or not, our thoughts and interpretations of people and events directly influence our beliefs and, ultimately, our leadership actions. Henry Ford once said, "Whether you think you can or cannot, you're right." In other words, what we think is what we get.

Hannah Teeter understands this. While most girls were playing with dolls or getting ready for their high school proms, Hannah, Olympic gold medalist in the half-pipe snowboarding event, was trying to keep up with her four older brothers. She learned whatever they were willing to teach her about snowboarding, and they urged her to "push higher" and "go big."

After standing atop the highest step on the medalists' podium in

Torino, Italy, Hanna was interviewed by a television commentator. He asked Hannah, "To what do you attribute your gold medal performance at the young age of 19?"

"My secret sauce," she said, "is my brothers, having great parents and being able to stay positive about anything and everything that's come my way. Keeping a positive outlook is definitely key to success on a snowboard or in any competition."

Hannah is right.

An attitude of excellence is the secret sauce for today's successful leader. Excellent leaders mentally reframe situations to help their teams view challenges in a positive light...they take a new picture. Facts are facts, but the view we take is our choice.

Our experiences are much less important than how we choose to think about them. Our interpretations of experiences either limit or enable our future success. Here's an example: A mission-critical project you are leading has "promotion" written all over it, but it bombs – it's over budget, past its deadline...the works. How we choose to interpret those facts is how we shape our future. Am I a failure, a poor leader who is maxed out and on the way out? Or am I a great leader in the making who is learning some tough lessons that will help ensure success on the next project when my true colors will really show?

Ed Zander chose his view when he took over as CEO of Motorola. His first order of business was to turn around the $37 billion communications giant...to recover its excellence and its leadership in one of the fastest-moving markets on the world's business horizon.

What did this process require? A "nothing but excellence" level of commitment.

"One of my challenges at Motorola is to get this thing moving a heck of a lot faster than it is today," Zander explained.

Just a few years prior to Zander's appointment as CEO, red ink was gushing from every corporate pore and Motorola was headed for life support. Known for inventing the cell phone and a string of other major innovations in its 75-year history, Motorola had been struggling under the burden of older technology.

Zander felt pressure to "clean house" upon his arrival. He heard, "You gotta come in and fire everyone and get your own team. It is easier if you bring in people you know." Instead, his defining moment came when he decided to expect excellence from the existing leadership team. With only a few exceptions, he kept the same team and instilled a commitment to excellence in them and throughout the organization. Zander took the more difficult and longer path to change, but building sustained, team commitment is like that – there's no shortcut or easy path.

Even in the face of downsizing 60,000 of Motorola's 150,000 employees, Zander stayed focused on the excellence that could be. His next move was to jumpstart new technology and innovation that led to the company's rebirth – the launch of the ultra cool and ultra thin Razr cell phone. This was followed by its first iTunes-compatible cell phone – the Rokr.

Bottom line: Within two years of Zander's arrival, Motorola's revenues were up 28 percent and its financials had made the jump from red ink to black.

Deep commitment to excellence never rests. So Zander isn't taking any time-outs any time soon. He says he still has a couple of years of hard work ahead of him before the turn around is complete and he takes Motorola to the next level. In the meantime, he's giving it his best…and expecting the same from his team.

At any moment during daily leadership, we can fall victim to our own thinking. Self-doubt and fear are the enemies of leadership excellence. Our commitments define us and our teams depend on us. The choice is ours. Think excellence…always!

• • • • •

"The greatest discovery of my generation is that human beings can alter their lives by altering their attitudes of mind."
– William James

• • • • •

Create a Compelling Cause

We often hear, "Make every minute count!" But count toward what? How do we know if they count? We have to measure our time against something – it's our purpose – why we do what we do.

One of the most powerful human needs is the need for meaning or significance. We all want to contribute to something that's bigger than ourselves.

The world of work offers great opportunities for people to connect with a purpose, a cause, and mix their own secret sauce. The reality is that people care less about working for a company and much more about working for a compelling cause. Without a compelling cause, our employees are just putting in time. Their minds might be engaged, but their hearts are not.

Meaning precedes motivation. Our cause answers the most fundamental question, "Why do we do what we do?"

A team without a cause is a team without passion. Our team members may achieve short-term results, but they won't have the heart to go the distance. We might find that their hearts are much bigger than their jobs. If we get our team inspired about a cause, their hearts will follow. Our cause forms a bridge to a brighter tomorrow...and we have to build it!

A compelling cause *is not* a project goal, financial target or strategic plan. Our employees won't get emotionally charged about a "10 percent net profit," a "20 percent return on investment" or a "30 percent increase in market share." A compelling cause *is* a reason to be excited about getting up and going to work every day – to dread Fridays and love Mondays.

Compelling causes come in all varieties – perhaps it could be to help others, to make the world a better place, to innovate or to win. Walt Disney's cause is "to make dreams come true." Coke worked diligently to develop its cause: To put a Coke within reach of every person on Earth. Pepsi's cause – to "beat Coke!"

Your team's cause may not be apparent at first glance. For instance, a company that distributes building products to homebuilders may not seem to have a compelling cause, but a deeper look reveals they "help make the American dream a reality." Now, that's a cause worth working for!

Excellent leaders don't wait for their organizations to communicate a cause their teams can commit to. They take the initiative to define a cause for their own teams. They are bold. They step back and look at the big picture.

Our first step is to consider how our team improves conditions for others. What difference are we making? It should stir the emotions. We must also keep our cause real and relevant because **people can only commit to what they understand.**

For example, a customer call center may have a cause to brighten the day of each and every caller. An information technology department's cause could be to improve personal productivity. For a purchasing department, it might be to ensure all company products are made with the best raw materials available.

In a recent discussion with a client, we talked about how a compelling cause can ignite a personal commitment to excel at a job. She was reflecting on one of her first jobs as a dishwasher in a hospital. But she did not recall her job as one of only a dishwasher. Her cause was "to help ensure a clean, healthy environment so patients could heal as fast of possible."

Wouldn't you be more committed to washing dishes if that were your cause?

Explaining a compelling purpose can not only create a defining moment for employees, but it can also ignite a commitment to excellence!

• • • • •

"Happiness comes from following one's passion.
Success comes from work that you are passionate about."

– Anonymous

• • • • •

Secure Your Foundation

I recently built a new house and discovered that leadership corresponds to the phases of home building. Constructing a house occurs in three major phases: foundation, framing and finish-out.

Building a team, like building a house, requires starting from the ground up. Our foundation, like our values, affects our team the same way all the time. Eventually, we reach the moment of commitment when we lay our foundation. The homebuilder is committed to a certain floor plan – the way the house will flow – once the foundation is set. The team builder is committed to *how* his team will flow and interact – their values.

Most leaders remember the first time they articulated their foundational values. I remember mine. I called them "Lee's 3 F's" – Focused, Fair and Fun. They formed the foundation for what my team and I could expect from each other.

Framing defines the parameters (systems and processes) within which each team member performs their job.

The finish-out adds the final, personal touch – it makes each house special and each relationship unique. Finish-out makes each person feel the house or team we built is their very own. As a result, they treat it with a sense of ownership vs. an "apartment job" they view as short term.

Regardless of how well-designed our framing and finish-out are, our team's house can only be as strong as the leadership foundation we have built…and our commitment to excellence can only be as strong as our foundation.

I recently saw a poster that read, "When the winds of change blow hard enough, even the most trivial of objects can become deadly projectiles." As leaders, we are the structural engineers who ensure integrity of our foundational values. When the storms of crises hit, we want to be sure our house is built on a strong foundation.

Sometimes cracks in our foundational values are difficult to detect. Our tendency is to fix the problem at hand. We see a crack in the floor tile, so we replace the tile. A bedroom door doesn't swing quite right, so we adjust the hinges. A window doesn't close flush, so we caulk the bottom to seal the gap.

Cracks on our team's foundation can initially look like a simple finish-out or framing problem. It's funny how we can find ourselves continually fixing the same framing and finish-out problems, but we do not realize these are symptoms of a deeper problem. For instance:

- Employee morale is dipping, so we implement an employee recognition program.
- Departments are not communicating effectively, so we have a meeting to discuss it.
- Personal accountability for results is eroding, so we restructure departments.

- The level of employee input and ideas for cost saving is too low, so we pull together a committee to look at it.

If we find ourselves dealing with the same issues repeatedly, we are probably not going deep enough with our solutions. What looks like an innocent crack in the wall (a small blip in employee turnover) could actually indicate a deeper crack in our foundation (employees see a disconnect between values and actions).

Leadership commitment requires us to fight for and protect our team's values. Cracks in our foundation must be detected and addressed in real time.

A simple and practical way for a leader to demonstrate a commitment to team values is to define the rules of engagement. These rules describe how a team will interact. They are like the "We Card." signs we see in every convenience store. Those signs were created to help the store workers.

In the past, convenience store workers had to ask each customer wanting to buy alcohol or tobacco for identification to ensure he/she was of legal age. This became awkward for the store workers. They had to visually assess who might be close to legal age (not a position I would want to be in). As a result, they had to risk the legal implications if they did not ask for identification from someone who was not of age. They also had to deal with the wrath of those who were offended by being asked for identification.

Today, with the help of "We Card." signs, workers only have to point to the sign. No fuss, no risks, nothing personal. It's a rule of engagement that is understood by all parties.

Defining the rules of engagement for our teams can yield similar benefits. They create accepted ways of interacting, so teams do not have to think about or debate what is appropriate in each situation.

Think back to your school days. Each teacher, usually on the first day of the year, explained the classroom rules of engagement: raise your hand if you have a question, request a hall pass to use the restroom, place your homework on your desk each morning, respect others' property, etc. These rules helped both the teacher and students focus on the most important things in the classroom – learning.

Defining the rules of engagement helps our teams (and ourselves!) focus on what's critical for excellent performance. They might address how to: make decisions, share information, consider ideas for improvement, coordinate handoffs, review work, challenge prevailing thought, prioritize and resolve conflict.

Our team values offer hints for appropriate rules of engagement. Our current challenges might also be a place to look for ideas. For example, one team who was having trouble getting all input on the table during their staff meetings defined these rules of engagement:

- Speak your mind during meetings, not after.

- We accept and encourage constructive disagreement as necessary to yield the best decisions for our team – nothing personal.

- We will present a unified front to the rest of the organization, regardless of disagreements during meetings.

- All problems must be presented with a solution.

Rules of engagement do not have to be wordy, but they must fit our teams and be embraced by them. Here are some other examples:

- All reports must be reviewed by at least one other team member before leaving our department.

- If an issue is not resolved after five e-mails, you must meet (by phone or in person) to resolve the issue.

- Customer-related tasks are always a higher priority than internal tasks.

- No team or committee meetings last more than one hour.

- Every project is debriefed for lessons learned within one week of project completion.

Excellent leaders keep their rules of engagement visible and apply them to decisions they make...even small decisions. These leaders also rely on their entire team to ensure each member (included themselves!) is performing within the rules of engagement. In other words, they lead and work by these rules.

Our values form the foundation of our leadership commitment. We must pour a strong and even foundation before we build a house to lead in.

• • • • •

"Leave no questioning in anyone's mind as to where you stand."

– Anonymous

• • • • •

Reflecting on...

A MOMENT TO **COMMIT**

- **Think excellence**
  - You are the conductor of your own thoughts. No one else can control them for you.
  - Mentally reframe challenges to view them in a positive light.
  - True commitment never rests...keep pushing.

- **Create a compelling cause**
  - Answer the question, "*Why* do we do what we do?"
  - Keep it simple and easy to understand – people commit to what they can understand.
  - Think big – your cause should stir the emotions.

- **Secure your foundation**
  - Define and live by your team's foundational values.
  - Look at repeat problems for symptoms of cracks in your foundational values.
  - Define rules of engagement to reinforce your team values.

"The difference between 'involvement' and 'commitment' is like an eggs-and-ham breakfast: the chicken was 'involved' - the pig was 'committed.'"
– Anonymous

2

A MOMENT TO PLAN

Taking time out

"It takes time to succeed because success is merely the natural reward of taking time to do anything well."

– Joseph Ross, Author

Several centuries ago, a Japanese emperor commissioned an artist to paint a bird. A number of months passed, then several years, and still no painting was brought to the palace. Finally, the emperor became so exasperated; he went to the artist's home to demand an explanation.

Instead of making excuses, the artist placed a blank canvas on the easel. In less than an hour, he completed a painting that was nothing short of brilliant. When the emperor asked the reason for the delay, the artist showed him armloads of drawings of feathers, wings, heads and feet. Then he explained himself. All of this research and study had been necessary before he could complete the painting.

How often do we overlook the time it takes to prepare and to plan anything we accomplish? Just like the Japanese artist who took years and years to research, study and practice drawing and painting the details of the brilliant bird that eventually resulted on his canvas… any goal, anything worth accomplishing takes planning and preparation.

In today's warp-speed pace of business, planning and preparing are often the two steps that tend to get short-circuited on the way to achieving our goals. Add to this increasing speed of business the greater complexity of the internal systems, consumer markets, strategic alliances and distribution channels, and it's easy to see how the need for planning is greater than ever. In fact, planning is a **crucial step in every success and a requirement of all things excellent.**

The late Dave Thomas, founder of Wendy's restaurants, was the consummate planner. Given up for adoption soon after he was born, his adoptive mother died when he was five, and he spent the remainder of his childhood moving around as his adoptive father looked for employment.

Never having a traditional family, one of his earliest pleasures was eating at restaurants and watching families enjoying being together…a memory that would shape his later life.

In fact, in 10th grade, Thomas wrote an essay called "The Pursuit of Happiness." In it, he expressed that he wanted to own his own restaurant. To get there, his essay described exactly how he would learn the business from the ground up, then join the Army and get further experience as a cook. Thomas followed his plan to the letter.

After returning from his military duty, Thomas worked for a boss who owned four restaurants that sold fried chicken. As a result, he met Colonel Harland Sanders, founder of Kentucky Fried Chicken.

Dave's meticulous planning helped turn around four struggling Kentucky Fried Chicken stores. First, he reduced the menu to only a few choices, he used clever ads and added a rotating bucket as signage (if you are old enough, you'll remember those signs). As a result, he earned himself a whopping 45 percent of the business as part of a deal with the stores' franchisee. Once the restaurants became profitable, Dave continued carrying out his plan and opened four more locations.

By age 35, Dave Thomas was a millionaire. It was now time for him to implement the final step in his lifelong plan, so in 1969, he opened his first Wendy's Old-Fashioned Hamburger Restaurant, naming his business after his youngest daughter.

The subsequent success of Wendy's was also defined by one thing. Dave took a moment to plan each step of the way, and he defined a lifetime of excellence.

Planning is important leadership work because our product is a work of art. British sculptor Sir Jacob Epstein was once visited in his studio by the eminent author and fellow Briton, George Bernard Shaw. During their chat, Shaw noticed a huge block of marble standing in one corner and asked what it was for.

"I don't know yet," Epstein replied. "I'm still making plans."

Shaw was astounded. "You mean you plan your work? Why, I change my mind several times a day!"

"That's all very well when you're working with a four-ounce manuscript," replied the sculptor, "but not with a four-ton block of marble."

As leaders, we may not be shaping marble, but we are shaping something much more important and precious – people's lives and their livelihoods. Our product cannot be measured in pounds or tons. A leader's product has immeasurable psychological, emotional and professional weight!

A defining moment for the excellent leader is the day he takes time to plan – to chart a course for his team – versus reacting to daily, tactical demands. It's in that moment a manager becomes a leader. This defining moment has less to do with an official title than it does with a decision we each make.

Here are a few actions we can all take to get off the treadmill of reactivity and step into the zone of proactivity and planning:

- Set a high-definition vision
- Optimize your sweet spot
- Magnify your leadership.

Set a High-Definition Vision

About 350 years ago, a shipload of travelers landed on the northeast coast of America.

The first year, they established a town site. The next year, they elected a town government. The third year, the town government planned to build a road five miles westward into the wilderness.

In the fourth year, the people tried to impeach their town government because they thought it was a waste of public funds to build a road five miles westward into a wilderness. Who needed to go there anyway?

These were people who had the vision to see 3,000 miles across an ocean and overcome great hardships to get there. But in just a few years, they were not able to see even five miles out of town. They had lost their pioneering vision.

With a clear vision of what we can become, no ocean of difficulty is too great. Without it, we rarely move beyond our current boundaries.

Setting your first compelling vision for a team is often a defining moment. Whether or not the vision is ever realized, the success or lessons learned will shape our current leadership. Since most employees have seen their share of visions from plenty of different leaders, our best opportunity to create a defining moment for them is to set a high-definition vision.

The challenge is that we tend to fall short of providing the level of clarity most employees want and need so they can see the impact of their work. Leadership research supports this tendency toward a very low-definition vision. A groundbreaking Harris Poll of more than 11,000 households found that:

- Only 15 percent of workers could identify their organization's most important goals.

- A majority of workers (51 percent) did not understand what they were supposed to do to help the organization achieve its goals.

● Less than half of available work time (49 percent) was spent on the organization's most important goals.

In light of these findings, it's easy to see how a potential defining moment can be converted into a diffusing moment. Understandably, in today's world of work, taking the time to set a high-definition vision can easily take a backseat to other leadership demands that are "in our face."

It can also be challenging to decide what to communicate to employees and what to withhold. It's easy to say (usually to ourselves), "They don't really need to know all that," or "My team won't really understand," or "I don't think they can handle that news right now."

Remember this: **Leaders who *under*estimate the intelligence of their employees generally *over*estimate their own.**

Setting a high-definition vision is a "pay-me-now or pay-me-later" leadership proposition. If we log our firefighting tasks, we would likely find much of our time is spent on problems stemming from a low-definition vision. Our time invested in setting a high-definition vision pays off in less time wasted firefighting and clarifying the vision.

A high-definition vision answers the four questions being asked by our employees, whether or not we hear them. A closer look at these four questions shows employees are really asking us to explain:

1. What are we trying to achieve? (Goals)

2. How are we going to achieve it? (Plans)

3. How can I contribute? (Roles)

4. What's in it for me? (Rewards)

The clarity of our answers to these questions is directly proportionate to the clarity of our vision. If we forget to answer any of these or just assume our team knows the answers, our vision will become a blur of disconnected mega pixels. We will have a team going in different directions or worse, not even wanting to venture a few steps into the forest.

A high-definition vision helps employees see where they are going and how they can help get there. People naturally feel more accountable for their performance when they clearly understand they are a part of something bigger than themselves.

Take a moment to plan a high-definition vision. It will inspire your team to venture to new and exciting destinations with you!

●　●　●　●　●

"Man cannot discover new oceans unless he has the courage to lose sight of the shore."
– Andre Gide

●　●　●　●　●

Optimize Your Sweet Spot

Most types of sports equipment – a golf club, a tennis racquet, a baseball bat – have a certain spot that, if the ball hits it, will give the player the optimal result. Hitting this sweet spot yields a long drive down the fairway, a swift crosscourt return or home run swing. Every sport has a sweet spot of some type. If you have experienced it, you know when you hit the sweet spot, you barely feel it. The ball goes where you want it to go…even further and faster. Doesn't get any better than that!

But what about the sport of leadership? Aren't we professional athletes in our own right?

Those in professional sports practice 90+ percent of the time and actually "play for keeps" less than 10 percent of the time. As professional leaders, we are almost always "playing for keeps." So it's particularly important that we take time to plan and ensure that we are optimizing our sweet spot.

Did you know the average person possesses between 500 and 700 different skills and abilities? A common defining moment for people is finding that skill or ability that's right in their sweet spot. As leaders, we have a huge opportunity to help our employees find their sweet spots, too.

The first step is ensuring a good fit between an employee's natural abilities and interests and the requirements of the job. This would ensure the "highest and best use" of their talents toward the realization of our high-definition vision. Wouldn't we just love having every single team member working in their sweet spot? We would always be in "the zone" and work would feel like play.

Our ability to match sweet spots to job requirements is the best predictor of job success and, ultimately, of excellent performance. It all starts with a moment to plan for the use of talent on our team.

Let's not forget about ourselves in this matching process. Gaining insights into our *own* sweet spot as leaders helps us better determine how to design roles and deploy the talent on our team. For example, if my sweet spot is conceptually designing complex deals, I better ensure I have a strong analyst on my team. If my sweet spot is analyzing lots of details and numbers, I want some conceptual, big picture thinkers on my team.

Want to know an easy way to find your sweet spot? Look at the intersection of these two questions:

1. What am I absolutely passionate about?

2. Which tasks are very easy and natural for me to perform?

Most of us vividly remember the moment we found our professional sweet spot. Others told us we made it look easy, that we really excelled and we looked like we were having a ball. Think of the last time when others made these comments to you. What were you doing? Like finding any sweet spot, it's worth hitting these questions around for awhile and practicing our answers before we can serve up a winner.

Ralph V. Gilles understands this process. He dropped out of college and was spending most of his time – by his own admission – slacking in his parents' basement, eating granola, watching "Dukes of Hazard" reruns and lamenting the sorry state of automobiles being made in America.

Growing up, Gilles was typical of most boys who played with Hot Wheels and Formula 1 model cars. But, as a teenager, he also was extremely talented in sketching vehicles. In fact, his aunt wrote a letter to then Chrysler Chairman Lee Iacocca, saying he should hire her 14-year-old nephew.

A Chrysler executive responded, recommending three design schools. Soon afterward, however, the letter was lost and forgotten. Meanwhile, the car-crazy Gilles completed high school and enrolled in college to study engineering, but dropped out quickly. His reason: "I was in a funk and was really not sure I wanted to be an engineer."

As he continued his granola, "Dukes of Hazard" routine down in the basement, Ralph's older brother, Max, recalled the letter from Chrysler. He remembered that one of the recommended schools was Detroit's College for Creative Studies. Upset to see Ralph wasting his time and talent, Max pushed his brother to apply to the local school although the application deadline was only a week away and would require 10 sketches.

At that point, the whole family became involved, making Ralph coffee so he could complete his sketches, cheering him on and helping wherever they could. By the end of the week, Ralph was covered in pencil lead, but the sketches were complete, so his mother sent the packet to the school by overnight delivery.

Today, Ralph V. Gilles is recognized as the innovator of the Chrysler 300 sedan and the Dodge Magnum Wagon I in addition to being responsible for the 2002 Jeep Liberty, 2003 Dodge Viper SRT-10 and several concept cars. Dubbed as the Chrysler Group's newest darling, Gilles has earned numerous national and international

accolades. He has since been promoted to Design Director
for Chrysler.

If we consistently misidentify sweet spots, we will find our team
stuck in a funk, like Gilles.

If we correctly match employee's sweet spots to the job requirements,
we will all be living the sweet life!

Today's fast-paced, efficiency-minded organizations make it especially
challenging for leaders to always ensure a good fit. It's common to
find employees picking up the slack for positions that have been
eliminated. If personnel reductions aren't executed carefully, the
remaining employees can find themselves *under*employed – consumed
by "leftover" tasks that drain their time but don't tap their minds.

These situations start a cycle of "lowest and worst use" of talent,
resulting in a downward spiral of self-doubt, anxiety and frustration.
If you've ever experienced this, you know it feels more like a sour
patch than a sweet spot.

To prevent this cycle and the resulting decline in team performance,
we can plan the work for our teams to optimize sweet spots by:

- Combining tasks that require similar skill levels, so we
  can more easily match an employee's sweet spot with the
  position's requirements.

- Automating repetitive tasks.

- Streamlining inefficient processes and eliminating redundant
  tasks that rob us of getting the highest and best use of
  our talent.

- Outsourcing tasks that require a high level of people power but have little impact on our organizations. Stay within our own sweet spots and let other vendors use their sweet spot to serve us.

Take a moment to optimize the sweet spots on your team... including your own. It's a defining moment for most people when they can arrive at work on Monday morning and say, "How sweet it is!"

● ● ● ● ●

"The same man cannot be skilled in everything; each has his special excellence."

– Euripides

● ● ● ● ●

Magnify Your Leadership

Try holding a magnifying glass over a flammable object on the hottest day of the year. As long as you keep moving the glass, you will never start a fire, but when you hold the magnifying glass steady and concentrate the sun's energy on a specific point, it will begin burning quickly. The glass magnifies the power of the sun, just as it is our task to magnify the impact of our leadership.

Keeping things simple actually helps us magnify our leadership. Complexity eats profits – it's the enemy of excellence. For example, a study of 39 mid-sized companies found that only one characteristic differentiated the winners from the less successful companies: *simplicity*. Winners sold fewer products, had fewer customers, and worked with fewer suppliers than other companies in the same industry that were less profitable. This study found that simple, focused operations were more profitable.

The 80/20 Principle helps explain the power of simplicity and how we can use it to magnify our leadership. The 80/20 Principle is pervasive in our world:

- 80 percent of traffic jams occur on 20 percent of roads.

- 80 percent of beer is consumed by 20 percent of drinkers.

- 20 percent of our clothes will be worn 80 percent of the time.

- 80 percent of our e-mails are from 20 percent of the senders. (Go ahead, check your inbox!)

The 80/20 Principle is also alive and well in business:

- 80 percent of profits come from 20 percent of customers/products/regions.

- 80 percent of problems are generated by 20 percent of the employees.

- 80 percent of sales are generated by 20 percent of salespeople.

- 20 percent of your stock takes up 80 percent of your warehouse space and 80 percent of your stock comes from 20 percent of your suppliers.

If the 80/20 Principle exists in your business, then **the most profitable 1/5 of your business is 16 times more profitable than the remaining 4/5.** A bit mind boggling isn't it? As comedian Steven Wright says, "It's not an optical illusion. It just looks like one."

Let's say your company sells 10 different products (or services) that generate an average of $10,000 in sales per month. With the 80/20 Principle at work, two products would generate $8,000 in monthly sales ($4,000 per product) and the remaining eight products would generate $2,000 in monthly sales ($250 per product).

With these calculations, it becomes clear that the monthly sales per product for the top two products ($4,000) is 16 times greater than the $250/product generated by the remaining eight products. This same math works for production per employee, units produced, profitability, etc.

The 80/20 Principle should serve as a daily reminder to focus 80 percent of your time and energy on the 20 percent of your work that is really important. Don't just "work smart," work smart on the right things.

So how do we use this 16x magnification to create defining results for our teams?

First, focus on the "vital few" – the 20 percent that has the greatest impact. Do not only rely on your instincts to identify your vital few – use data to determine the truth about your team's performance. Look at customers, services, products, processes and people to find the 20 percent that drive the majority of your productivity, activity, waste, conflict or down time.

For example, you may find that only a few types of errors cause 80 percent of the rework or that a few team members produce 80 percent of your team's output. You may also discover that a small number of the services generate 80 percent of your profit or a particular department causes 80 percent of the conflict your team spends its energy on.

Second, once you have identified your vital few, create ways to leverage the ones that help your team be more productive. Look for the evolving vital few while they are still small. It's like investing in an undervalued stock before the entire market catches on. Leveraging small positive trends before they become big, and noticed by everyone else, offers a huge opportunity for leaders to make something really big out of something small.

Third, involve your team in eliminating, minimizing or automating the *trivial many* (the 80 percent) that hinder your team's productivity. Consider reallocating resources from your trivial many to your vital few – from low-margin products to high-margin products or from low-volume customers to high-volume customers. Take a moment to plan and avoid throwing good money after bad.

There are always a few things that are much more important or productive than most other things. Plan to leverage those vital few and magnify your leadership 16x!

• • • • •

"Your goal is to enable and empower people to make decisions independent of you. Each person on your team is an extension of your leadership. If they feel empowered by you, they will magnify your power to lead."
– Tom Ridge, former Secretary of Homeland Security

• • • • •

Reflecting on...

A Moment to **PLAN**

● **Set a high-definition vision**

  ○ Answer the four questions employees ask:

    1. What are we trying to achieve? (Goals)

    2. How are we going to achieve it? (Plans)

    3. How can I contribute? (Roles)

    4. What's in it for me? (Rewards)

  ○ Be more specific than you think you need to be.

  ○ Don't underestimate the intelligence of your employees.

● **Optimize your sweet spot**

  ○ Know your own leadership sweet spot by answering:

    1. What am I absolutely passionate about?

    2. Which tasks are very easy and natural for me to perform?

  ○ Match each employee's sweet spot to job requirements.

  ○ Redesign work to keep your team in their sweet spots.

● **Optimize your sweet spot**

  ○ Cut through the complexities of your operation and keep it simple.

  ○ Determine where the 80/20 Principle exists.

  ○ Leverage your vital few and minimize your trivial many.

"It takes time for a fruit to mature and acquire sweetness and become eatable; time is a prime factor for most good fortunes."
– from the Atharva Veda

3

A MOMENT TO ACT

Making every minute count

*"It's not the hours we put in on the job
but what we put into the hours that counts."*
– Sydney Madwed

Picture this – at birth, all you have is a jar of 27,375 jellybeans – one for every day of an average 75-year life expectancy.

Since that first day, you've taken a jellybean out with each passing day. By the time you are 21 and ready for your first full-time job or to begin your career, you have used up 7,665 jellybeans, leaving only 19,710 pieces in the jar of your life.

Over our lifetime, we'll spend approximately 28 years sleeping, 25 years working, 14 years watching TV, 8 years eating, 7.5 years in leisure or miscellaneous activities and 3.5 years getting dressed.

Our lives are a countdown. Time is our most precious resource. It's all we have. Whether prisoner or prince, world leader or struggling citizen, we each have the same amount of time to excel.

Once we lose it, we never get it back. As a result, life rewards those who seize their time and take action.

Sometimes our actions get lost in our intentions. Have you ever heard someone say, "I intended to tell her how important she is to our team before she left," or "I intended to volunteer last weekend," or "I meant to vote this past election," or "I intended to keep my commitment, but...?" Well, the truth is, we judge ourselves by our intentions, but others judge us by our actions.

I remember talking with a good friend who was 30 years old at the time. He really regretted never going to medical school but still carried a passion for being a doctor. One night, he started his familiar lamenting, "Well, it was just a dream. It's too late now. It takes at least five years and I will be 35 years old by the time I am finished with medical school." I then asked, "How old will you be in five years if you don't go to medical school?"

My friend understood the point. In five years, he would be 35 years old whether or not he acted upon his dream. At that moment, he decided to make every minute count.

Life's rewards – a winning team, loving relationships, meaningful work, financial security, time to recreate, leaving a lasting legacy – come to those who *act* to bring them about, although life isn't always easy and there are plenty of excuses *not* to excel. **Excellence belongs to those who let their actions rise above their excuses.**

Here is a poetic reminder of the value of every minute.

To realize the value of four years, ask a graduate.

To realize the value of one year, ask a student who has failed a final exam.

To realize the value of one month, ask a mother who has given birth to a premature baby.

To realize the value of one week, ask an editor of a weekly newspaper.

To realize the value of one hour, ask a job candidate waiting for his interview.

To realize the value of one minute, ask a person who has missed the train, bus or plane.

To realize the value of one second, ask a person who has survived an accident.

To realize the value of one millisecond, ask the person who has won a silver medal in the Olympics.

Time waits for no one.

Treasure every minute you have and define every moment you can!

Here are three ways to seize a moment to act:

- Check your focus
- Treasure your precious resources
- Make real-time decisions.

"When we acknowledge that all of life is sacred and that each act is an act of choice and, therefore, sacred, then life is a sacred dance lived consciously each moment. When we live at this level, we participate in the creation of a better world."
– Scout Cloud Lee

Check Your Focus

At the beginning of my career, I remember asking my boss why, when the rest of us couldn't see daylight, he could see the light at the end of the tunnel and it was always coming from a rainbow?

"The simple answer is from a lesson I learned long ago," came his response. "The more you focus on the 'positive side of life,' the more you will attract the same things. **The things we focus on create a magnet for our lives.**"

As my years since then have taught me, my old boss was certainly correct. Focus on forgiveness and we will find the world forgiving. Focus on the comedy life offers and our lives will be full of laughs. Focus on opportunities and doors seem to open.

On the other hand, if we focus on the drama life offers – well, the kids today have a saying that fits perfectly: "Just save the drama for your mama" because nobody wants more drama than life serves up on its own.

More than occasionally I have heard (with not-so-subtle envy), "That guy really seems to get all the lucky breaks." I typically respond with a question, "Do you think he is really lucky or just focused on excellence?"

The truth is that being "lucky" doesn't have much to do with luck at all. The most successful people create their own luck. They appear lucky because their focus and preparation have put them in the right place to make good things happen. The timing is never right unless you are prepared to seize the moment. Luck is preparation meeting opportunity.

Have *you* ever wondered why some people seem to have all the luck? Maybe you are one of the "lucky" ones. In general, "lucky" people achieve excellence by focusing on:

Forgiveness	vs.	Anger
Others	vs.	Self
Opportunities	vs.	Problems
Gratitude	vs.	Envy
Abundance	vs.	Scarcity
Today	vs.	Yesterday
Building up	vs.	Breaking down
Humor	vs.	Drama
Giving	vs.	Taking

To check our focus, we can look at how we spend our time. Is it mostly on the right- or left-hand column? Your answer will tell us if luck is in your future.

When British entrepreneur Richard Branson talks about "luck," it's usually within the context of the records he has broken in hot air balloon flights and the lucky landings that followed, but many would say he's also been lucky in his business dealings, which go as far back as his teen years.

Like many of today's successful leaders, Branson started his preparation as a successful entrepreneur by accumulating business savvy during high school when he started publishing a student magazine. Three years later, that enterprise evolved into a mail order retail record firm and a record shop in London. In 1972, he built a recording studio and signed his first artist to his fledgling label, Virgin Records. Virgin's first album sold 5 million copies.

Branson's recording company went on to sign top talents like Genesis, Phil Collins, Janet Jackson and The Rolling Stones before being sold for $1 billion.

Today, Branson's holdings include 200 companies in more than 30 countries, including Virgin Atlantic Airways. Now a multibillionaire, Branson – since his first venture as a teenager – has also invested his time and money in several charitable foundations.

In every endeavor, Branson has made his own luck with intense preparation and positive focus. If we look for excellence in all we do, then excellence will find us.

Lucky leaders are skilled at creating, noticing and acting upon chance opportunities. They do this in various ways. One powerful way is to remain open to new experiences. When people become aware of something – a problem, an opportunity to excel or a defining moment – they tend to see more of that thing. I call this the *yellow car phenomenon*.

When was the last time you saw a yellow car? You might see a yellow car once a day or so. Now, for the next week check out how many yellow cars you see.

Since I have alerted you to yellow cars, you will probably observe many more of them than you had previously noticed. Is it because so many more yellow cars just hit the streets? Of course not. You just focused your mind on yellow cars, and like a magnet, you see more of them. First time expecting parents experience this phenomenon also. Having rarely noticed another expecting mother, now that they are expecting (they are now focused on others in the same condition), they see expecting moms all around them – amazing isn't it? It's the power of our personal focus.

Excellence works the same way. When we focus on excellence, we see more of it in our people, projects, products…it's all around us!

Lucky leaders also expect good fortune. They are certain that the future will be bright. Over time, expecting good luck becomes a self-fulfilling prophecy because it helps people persist in the face of failure and positively shapes their interactions with other people. They do not dwell on ill fortune and they take control of improving the situation…with action.

I like what Thomas Jefferson had to say about luck. Certainly, times have changed but the truth of his words has not. Jefferson said, "I'm a great believer in luck, and I find the harder I work, the more I have of it." Hard work might not only yield defining moments for our team, but it also yields defining excellence.

• • • • •

"You can tell a lot about a person by the way he or she handles these three things: a rainy day, lost luggage and tangled Christmas tree lights."

– Maya Angelou

• • • • •

Treasure Your Precious Resources

Charlie Jones is a sportscaster who has covered several Olympic games in his long career. At the 1996 games in Atlanta, he was assigned to announce the rowing, canoeing and kayaking events – a situation that left him less than thrilled, since it was broadcast at 7 a.m. and the venue was an hour's drive from Atlanta.

What Jones discovered, however, was that it ended up being one of the most memorable sports events in his career because he gained a chance to understand the mental workings of these Olympic athletes.

Preparing for the broadcast, Jones interviewed the rowers and asked them about conditions such as rain, strong winds or breaking an oar. Each time the response was the same:

"That's outside my boat."

After hearing the same answer again and again, Jones realized that these Olympic athletes had a remarkable focus. In their attempt to win an Olympic medal, he writes:

"They were interested only in what they could control...and that was what was going on inside their boat."

Everything else was beyond their control and not worth the expense of mental energy that would distract them from their ultimate goal.

Jones writes that this insight made the event "by far the best Olympics of my life," and it changed his thinking in other parts of his life as well.

We all remember the moments when we had to redirect employees' effort back "inside the boat" to keep our team focused. I remember having to jump overboard a few times to rescue employees who had drifted way outside our boat!

We can stay inside our boat by treasuring our precious resources. Our time, energy and money are precious resources – if we spend them in one area, we cannot spend them in another area. They are finite.

As a result, **saying "Yes" to one thing always means saying "No" to something else.** Communicating this message deep into our team enables employees to say "No" to non-value-added tasks and to stay focused inside the boat…on value-added tasks.

One important way to demonstrate a team's focus is to say "No" to activities that do not support it's high-definition vision.

Saying "No" helped Walgreens outperform the stock market average 15 times between 1975 and 2000. At one point, Walgreens owned more than 500 restaurants. They decided their future was in convenience drug stores and that they would be out of the restaurant business in five years – they redefined their boat. They courageously stuck to their commitment, which required saying "No" many times to ensure a redirection of resources to their new future.

Saying "No" also applies to the day-to-day decisions we make as leaders. For example, if we spend two hours in a meeting that does not help our team achieve its vision, we pay an opportunity cost by spending time on non-value-added tasks. If we find ourselves saying, "That was a waste of time," or "Why was I attending that meeting?" – these are signs we need to say "No."

Meetings are an important way to conduct business. When I call a meeting, I think about the salaries of each attendee and the potential time they could be working on other important goals instead of being in the meeting. Since leaders decide how to use their employees' time, they must ensure a good return for their time investment. Of course, meetings can be both necessary and useful, but they can also diffuse our focus if we do not know when to say "No."

Treasuring our precious resources to help our team excel might not only create a defining moment for ourselves as leaders, but also for our teams!

● ● ● ● ●

"Success is only another form of failure
if we forget what our priorities should be."
– Harry Lloyd, Actor-Director

● ● ● ● ●

Make Real-Time Decisions

No tape-delayed decisions here! Only real-time decisions build real excellence today. As we discussed in the previous chapter, planning is important, but once we have all the facts we need, waiting to make the decision does not improve our decision.

Take a look at this next paragraph. Go ahead, read it!

Cna yuo raed tihs? i cdnuolt blveiee taht I cluod aulaclty uesdnatnrd waht I was rdanieg. The phaonmneal pweor of the hmuan mnid, aoccdrnig to a rscheearch at Cmabrigde Uinervtisy, it dseno't mtaetr in waht oerdr the ltteres in a wrod are, the olny iproamtnt tihng is taht the frsit and lsat ltteer be in the rghit pclae. The rset can be a taotl mses and you can sitll raed it whotuit a pboerlm. Tihs is bcuseae the huamn mnid deos not raed ervey lteter by istlef, but the wrod as a wlohe. Azanmig huh? yaeh and I awlyas tghuhot slpeling was ipmorantt!

It's amazing how our minds are wired to make decisions, in this case decipher words, with far less than complete information. We have this same capacity in our leadership roles. For many leaders, it is a defining moment the first time they use their intuition to "fill in the blanks" and make a real-time decision for their teams, just as we filled in the blanks to read the above paragraph.

The 80/20 Principle can help us make real-time decisions – smart **and** fast decisions. Imagine sorting all of the daily decisions you make into piles – important and unimportant. Typically, only about one in five decisions will fall into the important pile. Don't hassle with or spend much time on the 80 percent of those unimportant decisions. In fact, try to delegate these. Focus your efforts on the most critical 20 percent of the decisions.

Go even further to apply the 80/20 Principle to your important decisions. Gather 80 percent of the data in the first 20 percent of your time available, then make the decision and act as if you were 100 percent certain!

We should re-apply our learning from 80/20 decision making. If our decision is not working, we should change our decision sooner than later. The real results of our decisions are a more powerful source of data than any hypothetical analysis we can do.

On the other hand, if our decision is working, we should double our efforts. Even if we do not yet fully understand why it is working – results are results. Of course, we should simultaneously try to identify the underlying forces of our success.

Our ability to make real-time decisions is directly related to how well we listen. Remember what Mark Twain said, "If we were supposed to talk more than we listen, we would have two mouths and one ear." **Excellent leaders listen at least 50 percent of the time.**

I have spoken with hundreds of employees who experienced defining moments when their boss simply asked them what they thought… then really listened. If we're not listening to our employees, we will gradually suffer from "blind spots" – weaknesses that are apparent to others but not to us.

Consider a classic episode of *Seinfeld* featuring Elaine while she was the acting president of her company. She couldn't figure out why her entire staff was suddenly shying away from her. She quickly blamed her friend George for her seeming downfall at the office. This all started to happen after a company party where Elaine, thinking she was a good dancer, did not hesitate to show off a few of her moves.

Unfortunately, this was a HUGE blind spot for Elaine. It was painfully clear to everyone else that Elaine was a horrible dancer as she flailed and contorted her way across the floor!

As a viewer, you could feel the tingle of embarrassment for her and the dread if you should ever find yourself in such a situation. Fortunately for Elaine, she had an incredibly blunt friend in Kramer who, in no uncertain terms, revealed her blind spot by saying, "You stink!"

Learn from Elaine. Listen to your employees, particularly your "Kramers."

Excellent leaders prevent blind spots by taking a moment to ask and listen so they can keep in tune with the realities of their employees.

This is particularly important because **the higher you are in an organization, the more filtered the information you receive.** It's a natural and predictable phenomenon, but it's also a precarious position for any leader. No leader wants to be "Elaine on the dance floor." Therefore, the higher your leadership position, the more listening you need to do.

When we ask our employees what they think and listen to their answers, we are equipping ourselves with insights that enable future real-time decisions. The key word is *future*.

We must collect employee and customer input on an ongoing basis, to have enough data to make real-time decisions. The information we have received enables us to use our leadership intuition to quickly act and make real-time decisions.

●　●　●　●　●

"An organization's ability to learn, and translate that learning into action rapidly, is the ultimate competitive advantage."
– Jack Welch, former CEO, General Electric

●　●　●　●　●

Reflecting on…

A MOMENT TO **ACT**

● Check your focus

○ Look for excellence in all you do and excellence will find you.

○ Look at how you spend your time to see if "luck" is in your future.

○ Hard work is the best predictor of luck…and excellence.

● Treasure your precious resources

○ Say "No" to non-value-added activities.

○ Use your team's time, money and energy carefully, particularly in meetings.

○ Define what's "inside your boat" and stay focused on it.

● Make real-time decisions

○ Spend your time on the most important 20 percent of your decisions.

○ Collect the best information you can quickly, then use your leadership intuition to make the decision.

○ Listen at least 50 percent of the time.

"If you don't make things happen, then things will happen to you."
— Roman Virgils

4

A MOMENT TO **CONNECT**

Reaching for the hands of time

*"Many times a day I realize how much my own outer and inner life
is built upon the labors of my fellow men, both living and dead,
and how earnestly I must exert myself in order to give in return
as much as I have received from that connection."*

— Albert Einstein

How often do you hear people speak with envy about companies with "real heart"? Companies like Starbucks, Ben and Jerry's, Southwest Airlines, Harley-Davidson, Enterprise Rent-A-Car, Nordstrom, FedEx and Saturn to name a few.

Outsiders are constantly looking for their "secrets" to success. The secret lies in the hearts of their employees. These companies create *connected* teams and, as a result, built dominant businesses by acting like geese. Like geese?

Well, next fall, when you see geese heading south for the winter, flying along in "V" formation, you might consider what science has discovered about why they fly that way. As each bird flaps its wings, it creates an uplift for the bird immediately following. By flying in "V" formation, the whole flock adds at least 71 percent greater flying range than if each bird flew alone.

People who share a common direction and sense of community can get where they are going more quickly and easily because they are traveling on the thrust of one another.

When a goose falls out of formation, it suddenly feels the drag and resistance of trying to go it alone – and quickly gets back into formation to take advantage of the lifting power of the bird in front.

When the head goose gets tired, it rotates back in the wing and another goose flies point.

It is sensible to take turns doing demanding jobs, whether with people or with geese flying south.

Geese honk from behind to encourage those up front to keep up their speed.

Finally, when a goose gets sick or is wounded by gunshot and falls out of formation, two other geese fall out with that goose and follow it down to lend help and protection. They stay with the fallen goose until it is able to fly or until it dies; and only then do they launch out on their own or with another formation to catch up with their group.

Nothing we achieve in this world is achieved alone. It is always achieved with others helping us along the way. If we use the sense of a goose, we will stand by each other like that. Geese are defined by how they stay connected with each other. Excellent leaders are defined the same way.

I recently had the opportunity to observe a tangible benefit of a connected team. I was touring the distribution operation of a national retailer who is well known for building highly connected teams of employees. As my host and I approached the receiving dock, I saw a young worker, maybe 20 years old, waving frantically to the truck that was just pulling away from the dock. He got the driver's attention and waved him back to the dock. Then he quickly grabbed a broom and swept out the floor of the rig, then just as frantically waved the driver off as he yelled, "OK, you're good to go. Thanks!"

Since I was there observing their work processes, this intrigued me so I approached the young receiving clerk and introduced myself. I asked Lance to describe what had just happened. As he puffed, he said, "Well, that truck is headed to our main store where one of my teammates, Ross, is doing a rotation. Ross has a new baby at home and has had a tough few months, plus he just started this new rotation and he's learning the procedures on the store side. Anyway, I just wanted to make it a little easier for him when the truck arrived. This way, you know, he won't have to sweep out the truck on his end."

Now, that's the power of a connected team! This seemly extraordinary act of service by Lance is actually the norm at this company because its leaders have taken the time to build connected teams. They do it because they, like other excellence leaders, believe it's the right thing to do. As a by-product, **these connections yield discretionary effort – employees willingly giving their extra time and effort to achieve team goals.**

When you witness these simple defining moments, it's easy to see the ROC – return on connection. Let's look at how any leader can realize this return:

- Look beyond your employees
- Cultivate your network
- Ritualize your team.

Look Beyond Your Employees

William James, the father of psychology, stated that a fundamental human need is to be appreciated. This idea is supported by many studies that show the number one need expressed by employees is *to feel fully appreciated for their work.* The bottom line: **We do more for those who appreciate us.**

Although leaders widely recognize the need for employee appreciation, it tends to be a blind spot. We generally believe we are much more appreciative of our employees than our employees think we are.

After interviewing 25,000 leaders, Ferdinand Fournies found the most effective leaders had one thing in common – they expressed a sincere interest in their employees. "Sincere" is the operative word here. Our motivation matters! If we appreciate employees in hopes of getting something in return, they will see right through us.

When I was a leader in a corporate setting, I remember thinking I was really good at appreciating my team. One of my employees would always come through if an emergency came up on the weekend – I really appreciated him, and I could always bank on one particular employee to take on the big projects and make winners out of them – I really valued her.

However, in retrospect, I realize that I really only appreciated their contributions, not necessarily who they were as people. It took a whole new level of maturity for me to understand that appreciating my employees as people was a win-win. Employees feel appreciated and as a result are willing to give more discretionary effort, to go above and beyond.

After an extensive three-year study of the critical variables for leadership success, the Center for Creative Leadership concluded **the only statistically significant factor differentiating the very best leaders from mediocre ones is caring**. People don't care how much you know until they know how much you care. This particularly holds true for employees and their leaders.

We need to show our teams we care by staying plugged in. Today's technology offers many options – Blackberries, pagers, cell phone text messages, instant messaging, voice mail, e-mail. Be cautious of overuse of these communication options. We work in a high-tech world, but leadership is still a high-touch job.

With all of these technology options, it's easy to find ourselves too busy for face-to-face interaction, but that's one of the best ways to charge up our teams. **Showing appreciation is not a matter of time and intention. It's a matter of priority and action.**

Research by the former chairman of Gallup, Donald Clifton, revealed workgroups with at least a 3-to-1 ratio of positive to negative interactions were significantly more productive than those having less than a 3-to-1 ratio. In other words, more productive teams had at least three positive interactions for every one negative interaction. (By the way, the same study showed the bar was set even higher for more successful marriages – the key ratio was 5-to-1.)

What is the ratio for your team? Is it 1:1, 3:1, 5:1 or 10:1?

Consider tracking your team's ratio for a week to gauge how well you are appreciating your employees. Look for moments to acknowledge your team's efforts and results. This is basic psychology – reinforce those behaviors that you want to see more frequently. Catch them doing something right…and do it often.

Demonstrating our appreciation for employees and their efforts can put them on the fast track to excellence. There should be plenty of opportunities since a Harris poll found that 65 percent of the workers reported receiving *no recognition* for good work in the past year!

We should not worry about recognizing our teams too much. To date, there are no documented studies of employees, or anyone else for that matter, feeling over-appreciated.

Great recognition can even come from a moment of spontaneity. A Hewlett-Packard engineer once burst into his manager's office to announce he'd just solved a problem the group had been struggling with for weeks. His manager, obviously grateful but unprepared, quickly groped around his desk for an item to acknowledge the accomplishment. He ended up handing the employee a banana from his lunch with the words, "Well done. Congratulations!" written on it.

Initially, the employee was puzzled, but in time the "Golden Banana Award" became one of the most prestigious honors bestowed on an inventive employee in that division. Now, that's going bananas with recognition!

FedEx is well-known for using a planned way to spontaneously recognize employees. They call it the "Bravo Zulu" award. Bravo Zulu is a Navy term meaning "well done." FedEx managers reward employees for outstanding efforts and achievement on the spot. Rewards include "quick cash" bonuses, theater tickets, dinner gift certificates or even a simple note with a sticker of the Bravo Zulu flag on it.

As management consultant Rosabeth Moss Kanter puts it, "Compensation is a right; recognition is a gift."

Appreciation is certainly not a one-size-fits-all need. It should to be customized to each employee, so we need to **personalize employee recognition.**

For example, being recognized at an all-employee meeting might trigger more perspiration than inspiration for an introverted employee. Instead, use the information you learn about your employees to present an appropriate gift, token or sincere expression of appreciation. Invariably, the gift will be less important than the obvious time and thoughtfulness that went into it.

Here are some simple ways to make recognition a defining moment for our employees:

- Say "Thank You!" – an all-too-obvious, yet highly underused, form of appreciation.

- Allow employees to present their work to *your* boss. This is a great way to engage employees, and it also shows your boss what kind of leader you are.

- Offer team members a choice of projects to work on. When employees buy into a project, they will put their hearts into it.

- Put a sincere acknowledgement in your company or department newsletter. This takes only a few minutes of your time but creates long-term "trophy value" for the employee.

- Tell an employee's story of accomplishment at a staff meeting. Detailed stories are perceived as more interesting, meaningful, thoughtful and memorable.

- Take a team member to lunch to show your appreciation. Remember to do more listening than talking.

The good news is that we have complete control over this type of recognition. No budget limitations or excuses here – there are literally thousands of ways to create defining moments at little or no cost. As we strive to make connections with our team and recognize them, our goal is to be creative and outthink our competition, not outspend them.

• • • • •

"Thankfulness is the beginning of gratitude. Gratitude is the completion of thankfulness. Thankfulness may consist merely of words. Gratitude is shown in acts."

– Henri Frederic Ami, Swiss philosopher, poet and critic

• • • • •

Cultivate Your Network

I use the word "cultivate" purposefully because when it comes to relationships, the law of the harvest holds true – we reap what we sow. We must methodically cultivate our relationships – they are our lifeline.

In today's mobile world, our relationships are often the only constant. Excellent leaders are also resourceful people – they know how to access their network to quickly get stuff done. Any decent contact management system can help store and update contact information, track interactions and enter other helpful data (birthdays, special skills, personal hobbies, spouse's name, etc.).

Simply managing contacts is necessary but not sufficient to cultivate relationships. Keep your network alive! Staying connected with colleagues helps us stay current with new trends, gives us ideas of where we might need to build our skills, and enables quick access to helpful resources when we need them.

Thirty-four-year-old futurist Andrew Zolli supplies the "Z" in Z+Partners, and his partners are a fluid contingency of people. He assembles the best in the business to work on a particular problem.

His unique consulting approach has landed assignments from GE, Sun, eBay and Target. His strength is helping companies understand what the next 25 years might look like. By providing this information, his clients can make better-informed choices and develop their abilities to deal with hurdles such as the post 9/11 economy, but his secret weapon is his ability to assemble made-to-order networks of experts.

These networks include academic futurists, Fulbright Scholars, ethnographic researchers, technology forecasters and many others. Together, they are able to construct possible or probable scenarios and what-if situations.

Zolli was named to *Fast Company's* "Fast 50 Under 35" in 2005. In that same year, he quadrupled the business of his forecasting, ideation and design think-tank and his influence continues to expand.

In essence, Zolli brings a team together and gets them flying like geese – all focusing on the same problem. He has made a business out of connecting people, and as leaders, we also need to make it our business.

The best leadership advice I ever received was about being resourceful – connecting resources to problems. A very wise professor once told me, **"The key to success is not to know everything. The real key is being able to plug up your ignorance within 24 hours."**

Initially, I responded with a chuckle since this advice came from someone who spoke 14 languages fluently, was a black belt martial artist and a racecar driver, in addition to being a college professor! However, once I let these words marinate in my mind, I appreciated how poignant and practical they were. It became a defining moment for me. I gained a quick and heightened appreciation of the value of being resourceful.

As a result, I honed my ability to quickly access talent and information, so I could confidently address any leadership challenge. This advice was liberating in that I did not feel like I had to be the expert at everything…or anything for that matter!

It inspired me to build a strong professional network of experts and other resources. It also spurred me to learn how to ask the right questions to help identify the real problem, so I could harness the best resources for the solution. Now, in today's hyper-speed, mega-wired world, the standard for "plugging up your ignorance within 24 hours" has been cut to 12 hours!

Use every moment as an opportunity to connect.

● ● ● ●

"People tend to work in teams, in a collaborative way,
in an informal network. If you create an environment like that,
it's much more effective and much more efficient."

– Jim Mitchell, author

● ● ● ●

Ritualize Your Team

The country's royalty lined up, side by side, dressed in their full regalia and crowns that identified their region. They stepped forward to pay homage to the leather treasure that is symbolic of their common bond.

The king then handed the leather treasure to one of his compatriots, who proceeded to swiftly deliver it to his fellow citizens from his region who were seated quite some distance from him. However, the other royal family did not seem to be cooperating in the delivery.

When the leather treasure was finally delivered, some of the citizens expressed their appreciation with applause and cheers while others shook their heads in disappointment.

What ritual have I just described?

> *... A football team scoring a touchdown.*

Our rituals create the fabric of our culture, and they are critical for defining connections within our teams.

Once we establish deeply ingrained team rituals, we view them as "the way we do things around here." For an eye-opening view of your team's rituals, try making believe you are a Martian visiting your team and take note of the observable team rituals.

We can create rituals around hiring, recognition, production, innovation, heroes, quality, promotions, family, customer service, community service, learning, etc. Whatever form the ritual takes, it creates connections. Effective rituals connect our team members to each other, to us and to our compelling cause. Select rituals that fit your leadership style and the chemistry of your team. It has to feel comfortable and natural to be effective.

Rituals can be as simple as: celebrating employee birthdays; hosting regular social events; posting photos of new team members and customers; ringing a bell when a big sale is made; or sharing a proud moment at the beginning of every staff meeting.

Yum! Brands is the world's largest restaurant company that includes Taco Bell, KFC, Pizza Hut, Long John Slivers and A&W. To start each staff meeting, they all do the YUM! cheer, and it's an honor to be asked to lead it. Everyone participates, every time, with everything they have! Trust me, I've been a guest during a meeting and have done the cheer, myself. Sound corny? Not at all. It is an energizing and fun way to connect a team and start a meeting...a powerful ritual!

Markeeta Graban, associate director of the Department of Psychiatry at the University of Michigan Health System, reports, "It's really true that anything can be a significant form of recognition. Over three years ago, I drew a star on a piece of scrap paper, colored it, and gave it to someone for helping me out that day. They, in turn, gave it to someone, who gave it to someone else. It took on special significance with each use. Now we have it on a magnetic backing and pass it on to someone who has helped or is having a rough day. People love it!"

During stressful times at Maritz Performance Improvement Co. in Missouri, leaders use the "Thanks a Bunch" award. Someone brings in a bunch of flowers to give a hardworking employee, who keeps one flower and a thank you card but passes on the remaining bunch to another performer who, in turn, repeats the process. At the end of the day, they collect all the cards and draw for prizes.

Team rituals do not have to be focused inward. Many corporations, large and small, build rituals around how they help the community, whether it's tutoring at local schools, helping with fund raising races/walks, visiting hospitals or working on beautification projects. Kimberly-Clark Corp. spent $2 million and had thousands of employees help build playgrounds in 30 needy communities.

Even America's low-cost retailer has a highly ritualized culture. For those of you who are unfamiliar with the Wal-Mart cheer, it goes something like this: A leader yells, "Give me a 'W,'" and the Wal-Mart associates (employees) yell back, "W." Each letter is, in turn, yelled and echoed back, culminating in the rousing cheer, "WAL-MART!" But the most delightful aspect is the Wal-Mart wiggle. Employees get to shake their booties to represent the hyphen in Wal-Mart, an experience that creates a brother/sisterhood bond among associates who are then overcome with the urge to sell and serve Wal-Mart customers.

Take a moment to connect your team with something fun, simple and meaningful. Keep it simple. Start with just one ritual, stick to it and don't compromise it.

• • • • •

"Much that passes for education is not education at all but ritual. The fact is that we are being educated when we know it least."
— David P. Gardner, University President

• • • • •

Reflecting on…

A MOMENT TO **CONNECT**

- **Look beyond your employees**
  - ○ Demonstrate an interest in your people, not just your employees.
  - ○ Ensure at least three positive interactions to one negative interaction.
  - ○ Go bananas with employee recognition – find ways to be creative and do it frequently.

- **Cultivate your network**
  - ○ Methodically cultivate relationships – they are your lifeline.
  - ○ Store information about your network in an easily accessible system.
  - ○ Use your system of information and people to answer any question within 12 hours.

- **Ritualize your team**
  - ○ Use rituals to reinforce your values.
  - ○ Choose team rituals that fit your style.
  - ○ Implement fewer rituals deeper.

"People will forget what you said. People will even forget what you did. But people will never forget how you made them feel."

– Anonymous

5

A MOMENT TO **INVEST**

Giving your time to improve a life

"If we are to truly invest in this generation of workers,
we must offer a brain to pick, an ear to listen, a model to follow
and, sometimes, a push in the right direction."

– Anonymous

Two young men were working their way through Stanford University in the late 1890s when, during the semester, their funds got desperately low and they came up with the idea of engaging Ignacy Paderewski, the great pianist, for a recital. After paying the concert expenses, the two students could use the profits to pay their board and tuition.

The great pianist's manager asked for a guarantee of two thousand dollars. The students, undaunted, proceeded to stage the concert. But alas, the concert raised only sixteen hundred dollars.

After the performance, the students sought the great artist, gave him the entire sixteen hundred dollars, a promissory note for four hundred dollars and explained they would earn the remainder of his fee and send the money to him.

"No," replied Paderewski, "that won't do." Then tearing the note to shreds, he returned the money and said to them, "Now, take out of this sixteen hundred dollars all of your expenses and keep for each of you 10 percent of the balance for your work."

The years rolled by – years of fortune and destiny. Paderewski had become Premier of Poland. The devastating war came, and Paderewski's only focus was to feed the starving thousands in his beloved Poland. Yet just as the need was most severe, thousands of tons of food began to come into Poland for distribution by the Polish Premier.

After all the starving people were fed and hard times had past, Paderewski journeyed to Paris to thank Herbert Hoover for the relief he had sent. "That's all right, Mr. Paderewski," was Mr. Hoover's reply. "You don't remember it, but you helped me once when I was a student at college and I was in a hole. You invested in me...now it's my turn."

Investing in other people, and ourselves, provides a far greater return on investment than the best mutual fund. Our investment in people is the best predictor of achieving leadership excellence.

Now, let's see what it takes to make this investment:

- Inspire future leaders
- Live your legacy
- Exercise your brain.

Inspire Future Leaders

At one time, Andrew Carnegie was the wealthiest man in America. He came to America from his native Scotland when he was a small boy, did a variety of odd jobs, and eventually ended up as the largest steel manufacturer in the United States. At one time, he had 43 millionaires working for him. In those days, a millionaire was a rare person.

A reporter asked Carnegie how he had hired 43 millionaires. Carnegie responded that those men had not been millionaires when they started working for him but had become millionaires as a result.

The reporter's next question was, "How did you develop these men to become so valuable to you that you have paid them this much money?" Carnegie replied that men are developed the same way gold is mined. When gold is mined, several tons of dirt must be moved to get an ounce of gold, but one doesn't go into the mine looking for dirt – one goes in looking for the gold.

Some leaders find themselves sitting on a mountain of gold, and yet they feel poor because they don't know how to mine the gold from their teams.

Excellent leaders coach good employees to become great people. They help them build better lives for themselves and others. They build their employees from the inside out...inspiring excellence at work and in life.

Although certain types of employee development require a financial investment (e.g., seminars, professional memberships, subscriptions), the best return is generated from an investment of our time and energy. When employees know we have a vested interest in their success, tough discussions become easier, issues are addressed rather than avoided and solutions are presented by rather than prodded from employees.

In the crunch of daily demands, we sometimes forget a fundamental law of leadership: If our employees are successful, we are successful.

Excellent leaders are crystal clear on this law and focus on nurturing success and inspiring future leaders.

When my son was 11 years old, he earned his Junior Black Belt in karate. Of course, I was very proud of him, for he had come a very long way since his first lesson. I remember that lesson well. He was seven years old, and one of the first things the master instructor taught him was a simple exercise called a kata. This kata ended with him, the beginning student, saying emphatically, "V for victory and bow for humility" as he crisscrossed arms over his head with fists clinched for the "V" and then bowed for humility.

That night, he came home from his lesson and quickly ran to me to proudly show me what he had learned. Seeing his enthusiasm, I dropped what I was doing and became an intent audience of one.

As he finished the kata, he performed the closing, "V for victory, bow for humility!" he shouted.

But then, to my surprise, he started yelling insults at me… "Man, I took you down! How about that buddy!" and so on. More than a bit shocked and confused, I asked, "Hey pal, what was *that* all about?" He responded in a very matter of fact manner, "Dad, that's the bow for humility."

Well, this pointed out how such a little difference could make a BIG difference – he thought it was a bow for humiliation, not humility!

Fear not, we clarified that definition before he earned his Black Belt!

If we depend on others' perceptions to meet our expectations, we will be disappointed. My son heard his instructor's performance expectation but made his own (incredibly misdirected) interpretation, based on his own perceptions.

The truth is we remember only 20 percent of what we hear.

Let's take a closer look to understand why this percentage is so low. Let's say I am hurried and swing by an employee's cube and say, "Ryan, please make sure you use the new format on the month-end sales report…thanks." Even if Ryan is a pretty sharp guy, what do you think the chances are he will hear my request accurately, remember it, recall it accurately when it's relevant, interpret my instructions as I intended, then perform the task satisfactorily?

When we look at it this way, 20 percent sounds pretty good, doesn't it?

Effective coaching minimizes re-coaching on the same topic. If we are coaching employees on the same thing repeatedly, before we get frustrated with them, we need to ask ourselves, "Am I inspiring learning or am I just checking this off my list?" "Am I handing off a memo with instructions or am I asking the employee to perform a task while I give him real-time feedback?"

As the list below illustrates, inspiring excellent performance requires time and effort. We generally remember:

- 10 percent of what we read (memos, books – that's why I have chapter summary pages to help increase your retention!)

- 20 percent of what we hear (instructions)

- 30 percent of what we see (looking at pictures)

- 50 percent of what we hear and see (watching a movie, looking at an exhibit, watching a demonstration)

- 70 percent of what we say (participating in a discussion, giving a talk)

- 90 percent of what we both say and do (simulating the real thing, doing the real thing)

In the example with my son, he heard his performance expectation (20 percent chance of remembering) but made his own interpretations from there. Well, this happens on our teams every day, and it's up to us to ensure effective coaching of our teams.

Coaching is a pay-me-now or pay-me-later leadership proposition. Take a shortcut and we will be saying the same thing to the same employee next week – no fun for either of us.

Excellent leaders invest their time on coaching right the first time, and as a result, they prevent re-coaching. Coach them now or coach them later…the choice is ours.

● ● ● ● ●

"Leadership is a serving relationship that has an effect of facilitating human development."

– Ted Ward

● ● ● ● ●

Live Your Legacy

In the early 1900s, Al Capone virtually owned Chicago. Capone wasn't famous for anything heroic. He was notorious for entangling the Windy City in everything from bootlegged booze and prostitution to murder.

Capone had a lawyer nicknamed "Easy Eddie." He was Capone's lawyer for a good reason. Eddie was very good at what he did. In fact, Eddie's skill at legal maneuvering kept Big Al out of jail for a long time. To show his appreciation, Capone paid him very well.

Not only was the money big, but Eddie also got special dividends. For instance, he and his family occupied a fenced-in mansion with live-in help and all of the conveniences of the day. The estate was so large it filled an entire Chicago city block.

Eddie lived the high life of the Chicago mob and gave little consideration to the serious wrongdoings that went on around him, but he did have one soft spot. He had a son he loved dearly, and Eddie saw to it that his young son had the best of everything – clothes, cars and a good education. Nothing was withheld and price was no object.

Despite his involvement with organized crime, Eddie even tried to teach his son right from wrong. Eddie wanted him to be a better man than he was. Yet with all his wealth and influence, there were two things he couldn't give his son – he couldn't pass on a good name and he couldn't set a good example.

One day, Easy Eddie reached a difficult decision. Wanting to rectify wrongs he had done, he decided he would go to the authorities and tell the truth about Al "Scarface" Capone, clean up his tarnished name and offer his son some semblance of integrity. To do this, he would have to testify against the Mob, and he knew that the cost would be great. So he testified. Within the year, Easy Eddie's life ended in a blaze of gunfire on a lonely Chicago street, but in his eyes, he had given his son the greatest gift he had to offer; at the greatest price he would ever pay.

Now, let's fast forward to World War II, a war that produced many heroes. One such man was Lieutenant Commander Butch O'Hare. He was a fighter pilot assigned to the aircraft carrier Lexington in the South Pacific.

One day, his entire squadron was sent on a mission. After he was airborne, he looked at his fuel gauge and realized that someone had forgotten to top off his fuel tank. He would not have enough fuel to complete his mission and get back to his ship. His flight leader told him to return to the carrier. Reluctantly, he dropped out of formation and headed back to the fleet. As he was returning to the mother ship he saw something that turned his blood cold. A squadron of Japanese aircraft was speeding their way toward the American fleet.

The American fighters were gone on a sortie, and the fleet was all but defenseless. He couldn't reach his squadron and bring them back in time to save the fleet. Nor could he warn the fleet of the approaching danger. There was only one thing to do. He must somehow divert them from the fleet. Laying aside all thoughts of personal safety, he dove into the formation of Japanese planes. Wing-mounted 50 calibers blazed as he charged in, attacking one surprised enemy plane and then another. Butch wove in and out of the now broken formation and fired at as many planes as possible until all his ammunition was finally spent. Undaunted, he continued the assault.

He dove at the planes, trying to clip a wing or tail in hopes of damaging as many enemy planes as possible and rendering them unfit to fly. Finally, the exasperated Japanese squadron took off in another direction.

Deeply relieved, Butch O'Hare and his tattered fighter limped back to the carrier. Upon arrival he reported in and related the event surrounding his return. The film from the gun-camera mounted on his plane told the tale. It showed the extent of Butch's daring attempt to protect his fleet. He had, in fact, destroyed five enemy aircraft. This took place on February 20, 1942, and for that action, Butch became the Navy's first Ace of WWII and the first Naval aviator to win the Congressional Medal of Honor. A year later Butch was killed in aerial combat at the age of 29.

His home town would not allow the memory of this WWII hero fade, and today, O'Hare Airport in Chicago is named in tribute to the courage of this great man. So the next time you find yourself at O'Hare International, think about visiting Butch's memorial displaying his statue and his Medal of Honor.

So what do these two stories have to do with each other?

Butch O'Hare was Easy Eddie's son.

The life we live today effects the generations to come. Live your legacy before you leave it!

In 1981, business leader and self-made millionaire Eugene Lang looked into the faces of the 59 African-American and Puerto Rican sixth graders who had come to hear him speak. Years earlier, Lang had attended this same school in East Harlem. Now, he wondered how he could get these children to listen to him. What could he say to inspire these students when, traditionally, most would drop out of school before graduation?

Finally, scrapping his notes, he spoke from his heart. "Stay in school," he urged, "and if you do, I'll help pay the college tuition for every one of you."

At that moment, the life of every student in the room was changed. For the first time, they had hope – hope of becoming more than their older brothers and sisters, their parents and their neighbors.

Six years later, nearly 90 percent of that class graduated from high school, and true to his promise, Lang made it possible for them to attend college and then went on to found the "I Have a Dream"

Foundation, which has supported similar projects in 57 cities, assisted by more than 200 sponsors helping more than 12,000 disadvantaged students with academic support and guidance through high school and the completion of their college educations.

As the Chinese proverb says, "If you continually give, you will continually have."

When we do good, we feel good. One of the most joyful moments for any leader is to pass the baton to someone we have invested in, and then see our values reflected in the new leader. **We were meant to give away our lives.** We must focus on living our legacy instead of worrying about leaving our legacy. If we do, we will define ourselves and others by a life of excellence!

In our own small way, each of us can create defining moments that last a lifetime. Investing in others is not about money. It's about time!

•   •   •   •   •

"The legacy of heroes is the memory of a great name
and the inheritance of a great example."
– Benjamin Disraeli, Prime Minister of Great Britain

•   •   •   •   •

Exercise Your Brain

A friend's grandfather came to America from Eastern Europe. After being processed at Ellis Island, he went into a cafeteria in lower Manhattan. He sat down at an empty table and waited for someone to take his order. Of course, nobody did. Finally, a woman with a tray full of food sat down opposite him and informed him how a cafeteria worked.

"Start out at that end," she said. "Just go along the line and pick out what you want. At the other end, they'll tell you how much you have to pay."

"I soon learned that's how everything works in America," the grandfather told my friend. "Life's a cafeteria. You can get anything you want as long as you are willing to pay the price of learning. You can even get success, but you'll never get it if you wait for someone to bring it to you. You have to get up and get it yourself."

Excellent leadership is not just about investing in others. It's also about investing in ourselves. Today more than ever, there is a cafeteria of learning available to us…and it's filled with the food of excellence. The great news is there is no annual membership fee to the Brain Gym! Traditionally known as the library or bookstore, the Brain Gym is now completely virtual. All we need to exercise our brains is at our fingertips, literally. But it's not just about reading and training.

The Brain Gym is anywhere we want it to be. In other words, our lives are our own learning labs, where we can build our leadership competence. We can find best practices everywhere. Watch the people around us. We can find nuggets of excellence from a father-in-law, a clergyman, a speaker at a professional association meeting, a fellow leader, our child's school principal, a Boy Scout's troop leader or a particularly helpful salesperson at a local department store. Observe, read, ask, listen and learn.

There are also lessons to be learned in everything your team does. Look for opportunities in post-project reviews, customer meetings, conflicts with other departments, changes in priorities, miscommunications and mistakes. Seize all these experiences to exercise your brain.

Keeping our memberships at the Brain Gym continually hones our competence...and **competence builds confidence.** Confidence is critical — excellent leaders need it and their teams want to see it.

In fact, modern studies on the psychology of peak performance have found that most great athletes, surgeons, engineers and artists build their confidence and competence by practicing visualization. Why not add great leaders to that list?

One study on visualization was conducted by Dr. Maxwell Maltz, using a basketball team. He had five team members practice shooting free throws in the gym for several days. Five others practiced shooting only in their minds, visualizing themselves shooting free throws and making each shot. After five practice days, Maltz staged a contest between the two teams. What do you think happened?

The players who had *visualized* themselves making free throws did much better than those who had actually *practiced* making free throws. Such mental training sends neuromuscular signals that can lead to a stronger, more effective performance during the actual event.

Visualize your goals and imagine exactly how your body feels when you achieve your goal. **Your mind does not know the difference**

between physical and mental practice. Visualization is the process that allows us to see desired results in our minds. Once we can see it in our minds, we will be closer to achieving it in our lives.

Another way to exercise our brains is to glean wisdom from mentors. Most leaders, like a curious child, are full of questions. A mentor is a great source to help answer those questions.

Mentors offer you a precious glimpse into their life's experiences. As your goals evolve or you enter a new stage of life, your mentors will naturally change. You may relocate or decide to pursue a different career path. You might grow to a point where you reach or surpass the proficiency of your mentor. Be prepared to end mentoring relationships (always with appreciation) and be willing to initiate additional ones.

No one person can grant us all of the knowledge and tools we require to maximize our potential. For the greatest benefit, seek out mentors with specific skills you desire to acquire. Maybe it's the company's top strategist, the salesperson with the magnetic people skills, the teammate who consistently wows the crowd with presentations, or the executive who everyone always wants to work for. Target their strengths and learn what makes them the best in their particular area.

In our quest for excellence, the most valuable resource may be sitting in the office next to us. If experience truly is the best teacher, then we would be wise to study the life lessons and expertise of a mentor.

Your mind is a muscle. Use it, keep learning and it strengthens. Stop learning and it atrophies. Take a moment to invest in yourself and exercise your brain!

● ● ● ● ●

"It's what you learn after you know it all that counts."

— John Wooden, Basketball Coach

● ● ● ● ●

Reflecting on...

A MOMENT TO **INVEST**

● **Inspire future leaders**

○ Mentor for success in work and life.

○ Coach well the first time to ensure learning and prevent re-coaching on the same skills.

○ Expose your team to a rich variety of experiences.

● **Live your legacy**

○ Focus on *living* your legacy instead of worrying about leaving it.

○ Give your life and wisdom away.

○ No investment is too small.

● **Exercise your brain**

○ Embrace lifelong learning.

○ Use your downtime as mental uptime – read, listen, learn, visualize.

○ Use mentors to get valuable answers to tough questions.

"We make a living by what we get,
but we make a life by what we give."
– Winston Churchill

6

A Moment to CHANGE

Adapting to the times

"We cannot become what we need to be by remaining what we are."
– Max DePree

Trees grow up through their branches, down through their roots and grow wider with each passing year. As growth occurs, trees eventually shed their protective bark to make way for growth. Humans are the same way.

Just as trees need bark as a protective shield while growth occurs, we as humans need boundaries to defend our vulnerabilities as our potential unfolds…but our ongoing growth depends on our ability to shed this "bark" of protection when it is no longer needed. In some cases, an inability to shed this bark will constrict our ability to realize our full potential.

But unlike trees, which shed their bark automatically, we have to determine the right time to adjust our boundaries, to "shed" these protective devices in order to create the space we need to reach the next level.

Is this process always easy? Not always, but we can periodically take the time to question our boundaries and to ask ourselves if it is time to soften our defenses and expand these boundaries or do we continue to need this protection.

The following is an excerpt from a commencement address delivered by Steve Jobs, CEO of Apple Computer and Pixar Animation Studios.

> "When I was 17, I read a quote that went something like: 'If you live each day as if it was your last, someday you'll most certainly be right.' It made an impression on me, and since then, for the past 33 years, I have looked in the mirror every morning and asked myself, 'If today were the last day of my life, would I want to do what I am about to do today?' And whenever the answer has been 'No' for too many days in a row, I know I need to change something."

Jobs offers a good acid test for assessing our need to change. However, the forces for the status quo are great. Initiating our own changes is definitely easier said than done. The following historical quotes help illustrate the forces of resistance that still abound today. All of these people said it couldn't be done:

- Everything that can be invented has been invented.
  – *Charles H. Duell, Director of the U.S. Patent Office, 1899*

- Heavier-than-air flying machines are impossible.
  - *Lord Kelvin, President, Royal Society, 1895*

- Sensible and responsible women do not want to vote.
  - *Grover Cleveland, U.S. President, 1905*

- Babe Ruth made a mistake when he gave up pitching.
  - *Tris Speaker, baseball player, 1921*

- There is no likelihood that man can ever tap the power of the atom.
  - *Robert Millikan, Nobel Prize Winner, Physics, 1927*

- Who in the world wants to hear actors talk?
  - *Harry Warner, Warner Brothers Pictures, 1927*

It's up to us as leaders to define our own future and turn a deaf ear to doubt casters, just as those change agents did who ultimately made these statements humorous and absurd. Here's how we can take a moment to change:

- Delight in discomfort

- Know fear

- Multiply your power of one.

Delight in Discomfort

Success naturally makes us comfortable. We want to enjoy our success, so we tend to slow down…just a little, we let our focus slip…just a little, we play it safe…just a little. It might be hard to see this in ourselves, but it's easy to see it in the world of sports. How many times have we seen teams lose their momentum and then lose the game because instead of playing to win, they began playing not to lose? They get ahead, but then they pull back and stop playing with the intensity that earned them the lead.

The same temptation traps leaders. As we exceed expectations and hit our targets, our team might feel like they are cruising for their best year ever. Then, all of a sudden, the focus shifts from gaining momentum to sustaining momentum. The moment leaders change focus, momentum vanishes. Most teams just can't seem to "run up the score" on their opponents.

The challenge is that we are all hardwired for comfort. My entire career, I have helped organizations and individuals manage changes and step outside their comfort zones. However, last year I received a letter from my bank, informing me that I would no longer be able to pay my bill via touchtone phone and I would have to move to online banking. Well, I resisted that change more than all my toughest clients combined!

I knew what was going on, but my hardwiring kicked in. Of course, like most changes, my resistance was disproportionate to the degree of required change. As it turned out, the new online system was a huge improvement over the old way I was clinging to. Is it the same way with most changes we finally make?

In business, the cost of not changing has much bigger implications than just simply changing from a touchtone to mouse click. The stakes are high. Leaders who "grasp the past" are quickly left right there…in the past. Leaders who seize the moment to change are catapulted into a brighter future.

Here are a few steps we can take to convert distressing moments of change into defining moments of change.

First, **find delight in your own discomfort**. The way to keep your momentum is to seek discomfort. This does not mean you are never satisfied with yourself or others. Rather, it will provide a healthy alertness of where you can improve. By delighting in this state of discomfort, you will be more relaxed and more likely to see creative ways to improve. In other words, it will help you stay on the offense and thrive versus playing defensively and merely surviving. By capturing this mental state of delighting in discomfort, you will easily be able to evacuate your comfort zones.

If we do not change, we limit our lives and our leadership. Leaders who "delight in discomfort" say, "If you are always changing, it never feels like you are really changing." In other words, delighting in discomfort makes us comfortable with change. It defines the way we change.

Second, **when you feel like you are cruising to victory, take a look around…but not only at your opponents.** Look for anyone, any team, who is the very best at what they do. Compare yourself to them. What are they doing that makes them bigger, faster, better, smarter than you? Excellent leaders are never satisfied, never complacent.

It's easy for us to look at those we are beating and feel pretty good about ourselves. Looking at those who we can learn from, those who might have better "game" than we do keeps us humble and focusing on improving our own game.

Third, **lead beyond the status quo – always focus on the next level.** Here is an acid test to determine if we are leading for the status quo versus the next level. If you can achieve your goals doing "business as usual," then your goals are not big enough and you won't get to the next level. Your goals should force changes, require tough decisions, and inspire bold actions.

The next time you are feeling comfortable, enjoy the moment... but for just a moment. Then, seize the very next moment to change!

● ● ● ● ●

"If we don't change, we don't grow.
If we don't grow, we aren't really living."
— Gail Sheehy

● ● ● ● ●

Know Fear

We live in a society defined by its insecurities. We fear the loss of our jobs, our health, our money, our relationships, our sense of control. Here is a sampling of some less common fears to illustrate how far human fears reach:

- Dendrophobia – fear of trees
- Chronomentrophobia – fear of clocks
- Pentheraphobia – fear of a mother-in-law

- Consultophobia – fear of management consultants (I made that one up!)
- Xanthrophobia – fear of the color yellow
- Blennophobia – fear of slime

You get the point. Fear is deeply imbedded in many aspects of our day-to-day lives. Check out the evening news. Many of the stories are posed to get our attention by playing on our fears. A headline that reads, "Are you poisoning your family at the dinner table?" is guaranteed to get attention. So is the one asking, "Are your children safe at school?" In fact, when I was a youngster, I remember my mother saying, "We can watch the six o'clock news and not eat or watch the 11 o'clock news and not sleep!"

Since we fear most that which is unknown to us, defining moments of change can occur when we choose to know our fears.

Fear keeps us in the background, convincing us we can never accomplish our dreams. It is the voice of fear that tells us to keep quiet and to stay within our comfort zones. Without question, it is fear that stops us in our tracks toward our goals and limits what we are willing to try. For many, it is fear that makes us lead a smaller life. But fear can also motivate us.

For Li Vo, the young mother of two, facing her fear of heights was the least of her worries one night in the 1970s. Looking much younger than her years, she had joined the crowd of teenagers as they marched through her neighborhood toward the harbor that evening. Her Communist neighbors hadn't noticed her slip from her modest apartment and into the crowd. Her destination: America.

As the group neared the harbor, she glanced carefully at every vessel they passed until she saw the ship that would transport her and her family out of Saigon and to freedom, a journey they had saved for and plotted the past three years.

Somewhere, from out of the crowd, her husband Hui joined her with their two children. "You must climb up," her husband instructed her.

As she gazed up at the looming side of the ship, her old fear returned, but only for a moment as she gazed into the expectant faces of her children. "Follow Mommy," she encouraged, hooking her foot onto the first rung of the flimsy rope ladder. "We will be fine."

As she slowly took step after step, she allowed herself to look down, only long enough to make sure the children were following. At last, she reached the top and climbed over the ship's railing.

At 2 a.m., as the ship steamed out of the harbor, loaded with new refugees, Li and her family were on board and safe, leaving their native Vietnam far behind. Counting stops at refugee camps in Hong Kong and the Philippines, it took almost a year for the Vo family to finally reach the U.S. and the hospitality of their sponsoring family.

Even today, some 30 years later, Li remembers her defining moment. It was the moment she faced down her lifelong fear of heights to carry her family to freedom.

Knowing our fears and facing them will free us also.

The acronym F.E.A.R. stands for "False Evidence Appearing Real." It's a true definition of fear. It describes how our minds can weave together false tales of how situations will turn out.

If I ask my boss about that promotion, I will get blacklisted. If I terminate Joan, I know she will sue us. If I don't nail this project, I will be off the fast track. If I don't get that bonus, I will never be able to afford our new mortgage payment. If I succeed at this job, I don't think I can take it to the next level again.

Fear is really a secondary emotion, not a primary one. Since we jump to fear so reflexively, we fail to think about our first reaction, which is the cause for our fear.

Causes of our behavior are easier to address than the symptoms, like fear. For example, our fear of flying might be a symptom of a high need for control, and giving up that control produced tremendous anxiety – fear. Our fear of public speaking (#1 on the world's list of fears) might be a symptom of insecurities – we are not expert enough or prepared enough to give a fluent speech.

The key is to identify our primary response to a situation or change and think about it. When we stop to think about our fear, we can determine if our primary response is insecurity, sense of loss, need for control or discomfort with uncertainty. Once we honestly identify our primary response, we start to know our fear more intimately. Then, we can equip ourselves with information and experiences to fearlessly manage change in our lives. **We must think about and act on our fear instead of simply reacting to it.**

This thought reminds me of the prison warden who told the condemned man to order whatever he wanted for his last meal, and he offered suggestions, "Lobster, Filet Mignon, Beef Wellington or shrimp?"

"No," the prisoner said. "I'll just have a bowl of mushrooms."

"Why mushrooms?" the warden asked him.

"I've always been afraid to eat them."

Don't wait until it's too late to know your fears. Fear is a natural reaction to the challenges of life and leadership. To grow, change and excel, we must face them.

Excellent leaders listen and watch for what they fear. They seek feedback and other signs that might tell them to take a hard left off a straight path.

Since the information leaders receive can often be filtered to some degree, it's up to the leader to get the full story. How do we do that? We can look for dissenting opinions, assumptions and perspectives to minimize our blind spots. If all we hear is "Yes," we should be careful. In fact, we shouldn't take "Yes" for an answer!

We can't wait for different opinions to come to us...we must seek them out. Excellent leaders seek "no holds barred" input from employees in meetings, one-on-one updates, surveys, e-mails, in the break room or even after hours.

One of the most common defining moments I hear from employees is the time their manager asked them for input. It's amazing how something so simple can be so powerful. By asking for feedback, we can create a defining moment for our team – we can redefine "how things are done around here."

Our greatest fear should be that we will waste a moment…a potentially defining moment.

Leadership excellence is rooted in a fearless confidence that what is discovered will pave a new, brighter path for the team. Know fear!

● ● ● ● ●

"We gain strength, and courage, and confidence by each experience in which we really stop to look fear in the face…
we must do that which we think we cannot."

– Eleanor Roosevelt

● ● ● ● ●

Multiply Your Power of One

All changes, whether it's a change in your team's processes or a worldwide initiative to end poverty, start with one – one person, one thought, one word, one action.

Contrary to the lyrics from a classic rock song, one is *not* the loneliest number. It's the most important number!

Many people used to feel that one vote in an election couldn't really make a difference. Well, recent presidential elections that have been decided by razor-thin margins have proven them wrong. **A single act does make a difference…it creates a ripple effect that can be felt many miles and people away.** Help one colleague, raise expectations for teamwork. Encourage one service rep, improve a customer's experience. Take one moment to help a distraught employee, build loyalty in your leadership.

This simple poem helps us see the potential of our power of one:

One
One song can spark a moment,
One flower can wake the dream.
One tree can start a forest,
One bird can herald spring.

One smile begins a friendship,
One handclasp lifts a soul.
One star can guide a ship at sea,
One word can frame the goal.

One vote can change a nation,
One sunbeam lights a room.
One candle wipes out darkness,
One laugh will conquer gloom.

One step must start each journey,
One word must start each prayer.
One hope will raise our spirits,
One touch can show you care.

One voice can speak with wisdom.
One heart can know what's true.
One life can make the difference,
You see it's up to You!

Don't ever forget how very important you are!

We all make a difference every day – one way or another. It takes the same amount of time to make a positive difference as it does to make a negative difference. It only takes a small act to turn someone's day from awful to awesome. **Our goal is not to change the entire world, but to change the world of those whose paths we cross.**

You change the world of an employee who you encourage after a tough day. You change the world of a customer whose problem you handle in a hassle-free manner. You change the world of your boss by sending him a note of appreciation. You change the world of the mailroom clerk when you ask about his family. You change the world of the person you let take the good parking space you could have had. You change the day of the store clerk who you look in the eye and sincerely ask about her day.

Tara Church is a living example of how small acts can make a big difference. Tara is the 19-year-old founder and past president of Tree Musketeers, the only nonprofit completely run by children and dedicated to changing the environment through personal action…the power of one.

Tara's transformation happened in 1987 on a Girl Scout camping trip when the troop had to decide if they would use paper plates. They had a discussion about the pros and cons and the troop leader began to talk about reforestation and the loss of the rain forests and how trees help to clean pollutants from the air.

Tara became concerned about the prospects of a world without trees, and she suggested the Scouts plant a tree rather than using the paper products that had required trees to be cut down. That was a moment of transformation for Tara. She could plant a tree and, in doing so, could change the world.

After founding Tree Musketeers, Tara worked continually to educate children and to change the environment through individual actions. By the year 2000, more than a million kids had planted one million groves of trees around the U.S. and around the world.

The next time you see a big, beautiful tree, thank Tara!

Another example of someone who multiplied the power of one is Roberta Torn. While taking a friend for treatments at a cancer institute, Roberta noticed many people awaiting treatment were alone. Many had traveled miles to spend a month receiving radiation or chemotherapy, leaving home and family behind.

After several more trips to the hospital, Roberta – a grandmother and great-grandmother – decided to try and make a positive difference in the day-to-day lives of these lonely cancer patients. Founding a program called Adopt-a-Friend, she solicited volunteers from her church and her neighborhood to adopt a cancer patient.

Roberta, herself, would adopt several, going to the hospital each day and spending time with those patients – and sometimes their families – who had come for treatments. She began carrying a bag with her, filled with toys for children, magazines, candy and personal hygiene supplies. Many nights when she left the hospital, she took loads of clothing home to personally launder.

When she decided the long-term patients needed laundry facilities at the hospital, she returned to board meetings time and again until the washers and dryers were installed. Then, she went to her church board and those of other churches surrounding the hospital, talking them into purchasing a complex of apartments where cancer patients and their families could stay at little or no expense.

In her more than 25 years working with Adopt-a-Friend, Roberta has not only made scores of friends from around the country and the world, but she has also attended scores of funerals and has shed tears with the families she has gotten to know. Now in her 90s, Roberta still receives letters and cards from many of her "adopted friends" and the work she began continues as patients still come for treatment and are adopted by volunteers who have followed Roberta's selfless example of caring for strangers.

Roberta Torn did not stop with the first change she made. Rather, she pursued excellence for herself and those around her – day in and day out.

As leaders, each of us must be the difference makers for our teams. Always remember the power and responsibility that come with leadership. We don't lead in a bubble. It's more like a lake. Each thought, each word, each action is like a drop of water into the still lake. Our thoughts, words and actions create a powerful ripple effect through our teams, to our customers…and beyond!

● ● ● ● ●

"Men make history, and not the other way around.
In periods where there is no leadership, society stands still.
Progress occurs when courageous, skillful leaders
seize the opportunity to change things for the better."
– Harry Truman

● ● ● ● ●

Reflecting on...

A MOMENT TO **CHANGE**

● **Delight in discomfort**

  ○ Keep your momentum by seeking discomfort...and delighting in it!

  ○ When you feel like you are cruising to victory, take a look around...but not only at your opponents.

  ○ Lead beyond the status quo – always focus on the next level.

● **Know fear**

  ○ Get rational about your fears – identify the primary cause of your fear.

  ○ Get to know your fears and act on them – don't react to them.

  ○ Seek out different opinions before they come to you.

● **Multiply your power of one**

  ○ Convince yourself that YOU make the difference.

  ○ Change your world with one small act.

  ○ Make a positive change every day.

"Change is the essence of life. Be willing to surrender what you are for what you could become."

– Anonymous

7

A MOMENT TO CONQUER
Standing the test of time

> *"Time is the cruelest teacher; first she gives the test,*
> *then teaches the lesson."*
>
> – Anonymous

Imagine this: You are a navy pilot who has been shot down behind enemy lines and has been captured. You have heard about this and seen it in movies but never thought it would become your reality. After your initial shock, minutes turn into days, days into weeks and weeks into months.

Every day is the same so they all blur together. You are told what to do, when to do it and how to do every single thing. The feeling of hunger has long past – hunger is just your new reality. The throbbing pain in your hands and feet from the 16 hours a day of hard labor is a welcome assurance you are still alive. Beyond the physical strain, your captors have removed any freedom of choice.

No choice of when you wake up, where you go, what you wear, what you eat, who you talk to, or what you do.

It's hard to imagine surviving in these conditions for any length of time, yet many heroes have done just that for many years. Their key to conquering these conditions? Even in the worst of human conditions – victim of a natural disaster, a criminal act, emotional abuse or even a prisoner of war – no one can control your attitude! It is the ultimate and critical choice we all make. **Real survivors are not victims of their own circumstances; they are masters of them**.

Our attitude is our personal boomerang to the world – whatever we throw out will come back to us. Express enthusiasm and it comes back. Offer a smile and it is returned. Start to gossip and that's what we will hear. Get frustrated about a team member and that's what we will see. Help a colleague and we will find a helping hand.

Our attitude toward life is the most important choice we make. Why is such a simple choice – embracing a positive or negative attitude – more challenging than it appears for many people? The bottom line is that we often forget we have the power to choose. We relinquish it, subconsciously, because we make thousands of decisions daily – and about 95 percent of them are subconscious.

The ability to choose is a gift, but it is also a *huge* responsibility. No matter what today's "it's not my fault" culture encourages, we are all ultimately responsible for our own choices. In fact, I like to write the word "responsibility" as *response-ability*.

As humans, we have the unique ability to respond. It is a choice we make, although many times an instantaneous or subconscious choice.

Will we be a victim or victor? The choice is ours. Let's conquer together and see what we need to do:

- Move through adversity
- Take your stand
- Stick to it.

Move Through Adversity

Adversity is not reserved for daytime soap operas. Even the most fortunate of us has experienced adversity of some type: loss of job, health problems, failed relationships, disappointments at work, financial difficulties, death of loved ones, etc.

I intentionally used the word *move* for this section. Since adversity has an uncanny knack of paralyzing us, it becomes critical to keep moving through it. Otherwise, we will be stalled in the grip of our adversity. Here are three specific actions that can help any leader move through adversity.

First, **take inventory**. When we are dealt a loss, we tend to think all is lost. Identify what is lost or changed and what is not. Then, express your gratitude for what still remains. **An attitude of gratitude creates happier, more resilient people.** In fact, more and more studies are showing that gratitude is the most common characteristic amongst the happiest people.

Those who have survived life's adversities will tell you – a survival experience is an invaluable gift because in adversity, you get to know who you really are. There is a Tibetan saying, "Tragedy should be utilized as a source of strength." No matter what sort of difficulties or how painful an experience is, if we lose our hope, that's our real disaster.

On a clear October morning, William Jeracki, a 38-year-old anesthetist from Colorado, was fishing alone in a remote area, when he accidentally dislodged a large boulder, which landed on his left leg and crushed it.

Knowing a snowstorm would hit by evening, Jeracki had planned only a brief outing, so he had dressed in light clothing and had not left word with anyone about where he was going.

Now, he didn't believe he'd survive the night, so he had to make a choice: amputate his leg or wait for help and risk dying of exposure – victim or victor.

After three hours, he pulled a pocketknife from his tackle box, tied off his leg with fishing line, and began sawing through his flesh at the knee. He sliced through tendons, nerves and his patellar ligament until his femur slid out of the knee socket. Once free, he crawled to his truck and then managed to drive the stick shift to the closest hospital, where he was then air-evacuated to Denver's University of Colorado Hospital.

Searchers recovered his severed leg, but surgeons were unable to reattach it. Today, Jeracki uses a prosthetic leg. After this incident, he went back to school to become a licensed prosthetist.

Following his escape, Jeracki said, "I'll never know if that was the best possible decision. But I'm here. I feel lucky to be alive." He took inventory and knew that although he had lost a leg, what he still had was really what mattered – his life.

After we take inventory like Jeracki did, the second step is to **convert turning points into learning points**. Use your adversity as a time to pinpoint opportunities to improve, learn, grow, rebuild or test your own character or faith.

The pathway to leadership excellence is not always smooth. There will be rocks in the road. Although these rocks might look like stumbling blocks, the key is to use them as stepping-stones — opportunities to help you and your team learn, change and grow.

Sometimes struggles are exactly what we need in our life — they define who we are. If we went through our life without any obstacles, it would cripple us. We would not be as strong as what we could have been. Think about how your own struggles have made you a stronger leader.

A young boy born in 1809 is a wonderful example of converting turning points into learning points to benefit millions of people. It was 1818 in France, and Louis, a boy of nine, was sitting in his father's workshop. The father was a harness maker and the boy loved to watch his father work the leather. "Someday, father," said Louis, "I want to be a harness maker, just like you."

"Why not start now?" said the father. He took a piece of leather and drew a design on it. "Now, my son," he said, "take the hole puncher and a hammer and follow this design, but be careful that you don't hit your hand."

Excited, the boy began to work, but when he hit the hole puncher, it flew out of his hand and pierced his eye! He lost the sight in that eye immediately. Later, sight in the other eye failed. Louis was now totally blind.

A few years later, Louis was sitting in the family garden when a friend handed him a pinecone. As he ran his sensitive fingers over the cone, an idea came to him. He became enthusiastic and began to create an alphabet of raised dots on paper so that the blind could feel and interpret what was written. Thus, in the aftermath of tragedy, Louis Braille opened up a whole new world for the blind.

The third action that helps us move through adversity is to **plan for the future, but live for the present**. Don't obsess about yesterday and don't be seduced by the promise that tomorrow will be better. In a speech to his students, a philosopher encouraged his classes to live in the present. "As mere mortals, we have no control over the past. It is already spent. We also have no control over the future. We have yet to live it. The only moment over which we have dominion is the present...and, as they say, time is fleeting."

I think my favorite poem says it best:

> Yesterday is history,
> Tomorrow is a mystery,
> Today is a gift,
> That's why we call it the Present.

The tragedy of Cantor Fitzgerald provides us with a poignant example of a leader who planned for the future but lived for today. Cantor Fitzgerald was the largest wholesale financial service company in the world. With 2,200 employees worldwide and almost 1,000 in New York alone, they were at the heart of the financial markets – the place where financial giants traded with each other.

On September 11, 2001, Cantor Fitzgerald, lost 685 employees, more than any other business located in New York City's World

Trade Center Towers. Chairman and CEO Howard Lutnick was late getting to work that day because he was accompanying his five-year-old son to his first day of kindergarten.

Just as he was leaving the school, Lutnick got a call, telling him that the World Trade Center building was hit by a plane and as he got to his car, the CEO thought it was something small, like a Piper Cub. As he drove toward the city, the bond trader began seeing smoke. "I just had to get down there as fast as I could," he remembers thinking as he raced down the West Side Highway, "to make sure my people were getting out."

When he arrived at the Trade Center, people were streaming out of One World Trade Center, where Cantor Fitzgerald occupied floors 101 to 105. As he got closer to the building, he began grabbing people and asking them, "What floor are you on?"

What he did not know was that his employees had their escape route cut off by the fire that erupted when the plane sliced through the building a few floors below. Among those at the firm was Lutnick's brother, Gary, who worked for the company on the 103rd floor.

Lutnick later learned his brother had placed a call to say that the smoke was coming in, things were really bad and he wasn't going to make it. He called to say good-bye and that he loved so many people.

Lutnick's employees, many of whom were in their 30s, had more than 1,500 children combined. Lutnick pledged to give 25 percent of his firm's profits to the relatives of the 685 employees missing in the tragedy.

In a speech several days after the attack, the CEO made these comments, "We will not allow this tragedy to sway us from our path – while we grieve, we intend to persevere. We remain confident that our systems and technology will perform as our customers have come to expect."

Later Lutnick said, "The tragedy publicly defined Cantor Fitzgerald. Internally, however, while it has shaped who we are, we continue to grow and change from who we were that day. We have been driven by our commitment to our families, motivated by our need to succeed for them."

Today, Cantor Fitzgerald has not only survived but is now thriving as a leading financial services firm in the equities and fixed income markets.

Said Lutnick, "The results have been beyond gratifying. The successful outcome of our decisions and actions in the days – and years – after September 11, 2001, offers insight into how we persevered through, and came back from, the worst of all circumstances."

Lutnick lived a lesson for all of us. In the face of adversity, he methodically planned for the future while he compassionately lived in the present.

Sooner or later, we all face some form of adversity. When it hits you, keep moving so you can conquer it and create your own defining moment...and success story!

● ● ● ● ●

"Press on…your defining moment may arrive just when you feel surrounded by adversity."

— David Cottrell

● ● ● ● ●

Take Your Stand

Taking a stand, for anything, requires courage. Courageous leadership is knowing what's right and then acting on it.

For instance, during the Nazi occupation of his country in WWII, King Christian X of Denmark noticed a Nazi flag flying over a Danish public building. He immediately called the German commandant, demanding that the flag be taken down at once. The commandant refused. "Then a soldier will go and take it down," said the king.

"He will be shot," threatened the commandant. "I think not," replied the king, "for I shall be the soldier." Within minutes the flag was taken down. The king was courageous, took his stand and he prevailed.

Former Australian Prime Minister Paul Keating identified two key elements of leadership – imagination and courage. He said, "Between conception and execution, there is faith, hope and courage. Leaders fail when they imagine things but don't do them. We have to be bold and faithful to ourselves."

Excellent leaders don't settle for what conditions force upon them.

As author Marcus Buckingham says, "The only thing that leaders have in common is leaders break all the rules." Excellent leaders don't just buy into what everybody else is saying, and they don't follow the beaten path. Excellent leaders are constantly creating their own conditions for success by blazing new trails.

Courage is doing something you are afraid to do. The word "courage" is derived from the Medieval Old French term "corage," meaning "heart and spirit."

Howard Schultz, CEO of Starbucks, applied this definition and took his stand when Starbucks wanted to move into a particular international market. However, Schultz was discouraged by every analysis he read, even after he spent over a half a million dollars on consultants, telling him not to go. Further, all of his direct reports were against the move.

On the advice of one of his gurus, Warren Bennis, he met again with his team, listening to their concerns and answering their questions and asking for their support. In the end, he had mobilized the support of his management team, and as Bennis had encouraged, he went with his heart, with what he thought was right and entered the market in question. Schultz stood his ground and, ultimately, was able to score another successful expansion of Starbucks into the international marketplace.

In today's world of boastful athletes, it seems that balancing courage and humility is a lost art. But the Winter Olympics offered a shining example for athletes and business leaders, alike.

For 14 days every four years, the Winter Olympics draws thousands of journalists to capture the triumphs of hundreds of athletes on the ski runs, the bobsled tracks, in the ice rinks and the snowboard courses.

Each medal awards ceremony connects with the public's admiration and national pride as athletes representing their home countries take the top step of the awards podium and that country's flag is raised to the strains of the appropriate national anthem.

Without a doubt, everyone loves a winner, but there are also a few winning athletes who use their accomplishments to focus the eyes of the world – if only for a moment – on the needs of the less fortunate…and, in doing so, display humility, perhaps, in its purist form.

When Joey Cheek, representing the U.S.A. in speed skating, won the 500 meter competition, he graciously accepted the gold medal and then made these remarks to the media:

"I have always felt if I ever do something big like this, I want to be able to give something back. I love what I do; it's great fun, but honestly, it's a pretty ridiculous thing. I skate around in tights. If you keep it in perspective, I've trained my whole life for this, but it's not that big a deal.

"But because I skated well, I have a few seconds of microphone time. And I know how news cycles work. Tomorrow there will be another gold medalist. So I can either gush about how wonderful I feel or use it for something.

"So I am donating the entire (winning) sum the USOC gives me ($25,000) to an organization, 'Right to Play,' that helps refugees in Chad, where there are over 60,000 persons displaced from their homes. I am going to be asking all of the Olympic sponsors if they will match my donation."

Cheek went on to win a second medal, a silver in the 1,000 meters, and elected to give the $15,000 bonus he earned from the Olympic committee to the same cause.

In a recap of the 2006 Olympic activities, one commentator mentioned Cheek's $40,000 donation. "It may be that Joey Cheek's humility on the awards podium and the contribution of his medal bonuses to a worthwhile cause may set the stage for more Olympic athletes to do the same in the future."

After the 2006 Olympics concluded, companies around the world had donated a total of $300,000 to match Cheek's contributions. Think: The Power of One.

Excellent leadership, in any venue, is about other people...not us. If we are fortunate enough to build a great team, we will all excel. Staying humble enables us to use our leadership platform to take a stand and conquer much more as a team than we could alone. Humility is not only a desirable trait in leaders, but it is also the fuel for leadership excellence.

Humility is expressed in our actions, not our words. We cannot afford to be like the guy who was a member of a nationwide, professional association of leaders in the workforce. He was voted the most humble leader in the entire association for leaders. The association presented him with a medal that said, "The most humble leader in America." Then, they took it away from him at their next meeting because he wore it!

Taking a stand requires courage to conquer the outside forces and humility to conquer our inside forces.

● ● ● ● ●

"I have found that the greatest help in meeting any problem with decency and self-respect and whatever courage is demanded is to know where you yourself stand."

— William Faulkner

● ● ● ● ●

Stick to It

When I was a senior in high school, I participated in a mock congress with fellow seniors from throughout the state of Florida in a program called Boys' State. It was a defining moment for me. Let me explain.

During the course of the week at the state capital in Tallahassee, we learned about legislative issues, primarily by acting them out and holding mock elections for a variety of political offices. So I figured, "Hey, I'm only here once. Why not just go for it?" So I ran for a lower level position the second day but lost to another student. No problem, I can take rejection. So I tried for a slightly higher office the next day, but I lost again. Now the stakes got higher – more prestigious offices on the line and a bruised ego that needed repair. I tried again but no victory. The next day again...nope! I have to win at some point, right? So one more time I submitted my petition, made the rounds, and cast my vote. Votes finally came and I kept my perfect record: 0 wins, 5 losses.

Well, now we were down to the last day of the program and only the highest offices were left to be filled – the Governor's cabinet. Here's where the real campaigning kicks in. Pressing flesh, addressing the issues, oh yea, and making a speech in front of 1,000 of my fellow students (most of whom had won some type of office by now). With five defeats under my belt, there was nothing much left to lose.

With shaking knees and sweating palms, I made my first big speech (thank God for podiums!) as I ran for Commissioner of Education. I decided to make perseverance one of my issues – it certainly seemed relevant, to me at least. All told, at least I left the week with a 1 and 5 record, but the one victory was the one that really counted. Even then, I knew enough to realize that, as Thomas Edison said, "Genius? Nothing! Sticking to it is the genius!...I've failed my way to success."

Unfortunately, most people fail only because they don't stick to it long enough to succeed. For instance, every year on January 1st, people make new resolutions. It is a time to start fresh, to implement new plans for various areas of our lives. But we all know what happens...about 70 percent of all New Year's resolutions last less than one month. Many last less than a week or even a day. It is not that our intentions are bad – it is just that most of us do not stick to it long enough to create a new habit, a new way of behaving.

Sticking to it long enough to win is a common defining moment for many leaders and teams. These moments are so memorable because they often test our faith in ourselves and our teams.

Since we frequently cannot immediately see the tangible results of our leadership, we must trust that doing the right things will yield the desired results. We demonstrate this faith in everyday things, but somehow it seems more challenging with our teams.

For example, I took a lot of pictures of our children this Christmas as they opened their presents. I took some photos with my digital camera. Then I started to feel a bit nostalgic. So I grabbed my old 35mm camera (call me old fashioned!), put a brand new roll of unexposed film into it, focused on my children and clicked away. This film was now exposed to the images of my ever-so-happy children. But if I were to open up that camera and look at the film, it wouldn't have looked like anything would have happened. I couldn't see one picture that I just took. The film would look totally black.

I know and trust the images are all there. I just can't see them with my eyes. The film has been exposed to the images of my children. The only problem is, I have not yet developed my film. Now, if I were to take that film to a developer, he would take me into a very dark, dark room, and he would slosh that film around in just the right solutions, and lo and behold, right before my very eyes, a miracle would occur. The images of my children would appear.

They were there all the time. I just couldn't see it until I got it developed. But the reality is, the moment I snapped the picture, that image was imprinted onto the film.

The life of a leader works much the same way. Sometimes, it might feel like our teams are going through their own "dark room" experience before we finally see the positive results of our efforts. Trust that your efforts will yield the excellence you pursue.

When Apollo 13's oxygen tank exploded, dooming the crew, Commander Jim Lovell chose to keep on transmitting whatever data he could back to Mission Control, even as the command capsule was incinerated on re-entry. Lovell apparently knew this final truth: If you're still alive, there is always one more thing that you can do.

The signature of mediocrity is constantly changing direction. The signature of excellence is sticking to it. Here are some other leaders in their fields who knew how to stick to it and excel:

- Fred Smith, founder of FedEx, was a student at Yale when he submitted a paper about the impact of a computerized society and the changes he envisioned for traditional distribution and delivery systems. Smith's professor returned the paper commenting that, "The concept is interesting and well-formed, but in order to earn better than a 'C,' the idea must be feasible."

- Country music star Randy Travis was turned down more than once by every recording company in Nashville.

- After one of news correspondent Katie Couric's early television appearances, the president of CNN told her he never wanted to see her on camera again. Now, Couric is the first ever female, solo news anchor for a network evening news.

Ray Kroc created such unparalleled success, most of us are unaware of how he really beat the odds and persevered his way to success.

During his entire life, Ray thrived on discovering just the right idea that would live on well after the man, himself. From a paper cup salesman, to real estate broker, piano player and, finally, milk shake mixer salesman, he always had an incredible amount of faith in himself!

At the young age of 52, Ray's biggest idea, McDonald's, was about to emerge. However, he had to muster enough courage in his new idea to mortgage his home and borrow lots of money to get it going. Oh! He wasn't a picture of health, either. Ray had been plagued by years of arthritis, diabetes, lost his bladder and most of his thyroid gland. But he never lost belief in himself. In fact, Ray was known to say, "The best is ahead of me," according to those who knew him.

Today, the McDonald's brand name is the 2nd most recognizable name in the world. Not bad for a 52-year-old with health problems, huge debts and tons of determination!

Ray Kroc was a simple man with a simple plan to achieve huge success. His secret sauce? Never, ever give up.

● ● ● ●

"Whoever I am, or whatever I am doing,
some kind of excellence is within my reach."
— John W. Gardner

● ● ● ● ●

Reflecting on...

A MOMENT TO **CONQUER**

- **Move through adversity**
  - ○ Take inventory of what is lost and what is not lost.
  - ○ Convert turning points into learning points.
  - ○ Plan for the future but live in the present.

- **Take your stand**
  - ○ Know your non-negotiables.
  - ○ Rise courageously above the crowd.
  - ○ Hang onto humility.

- **Secure your foundation**
  - ○ Keep the faith in your leadership – stick to it long enough to win.
  - ○ Ignore the odds and critics.
  - ○ Never, ever give up!

"God grant me the courage not to give up what I think is right, even though I think it is hopeless."
– Admiral Chester A. Nimitz

SEIZING THE MOMENT
A time to Excel

"How good is hot chocolate? You can only know if you have been outside, sledding, careening down hill about as fast as you ever want to go, until you've gone until you just cannot climb the hill even one more time, until you realize that your clothes are drenched, and coldness has gripped through your skin down to your very core, until you drag yourself to the kitchen, to warmth and sustenance and light. That's how good hot chocolate is."
– Anonymous

The pursuit of leadership excellence can be compared to the results of planting an exotic Chinese bamboo seed. When this particular seed is planted and nurtured, it can take up to two years for a sprout to break through the earth. It requires the right watering, sunlight, care and feeding so it can build a strong root structure and foundation for growth, none of which is visible above ground. However, once it breaks ground, this plant can grow over 100 feet in two weeks! The benefits of sticking to it are abundant with this seed...just as they are with excellent leadership.

One of today's most successful business people, Oprah Winfrey, nurtured her seed of excellence long before it grew to unparalleled heights. In fact, her company, Harpo Productions, is now a favorite case study for leadership in many business schools.

"To this day, excellence is my intention," said Winfrey. "To be excellent in giving, in graciousness, in effort, in struggle and in strife. For me, being excellent means always doing my personal best."

Her production studio in Chicago is many years and miles away from the farm in Kosciusko, Mississippi, where Oprah Winfrey was reared by her grandmother. It was there, too, that the precocious little girl "began her broadcasting career" by learning to read aloud and performing recitations at the age of three.

But those were the good years. At age six, she was sent to Milwaukee to live with her mother, enduring the rage of a landlady who didn't allow the little girl to sleep inside the house because she was black. It was also during that time that she was abused and molested and eventually ran away, at age 13, and ended up in a juvenile detention home.

Her mother, seeing she could no longer handle the strong-willed teenager, sent her to live in Nashville with her father, a barber who believed in strict discipline that included the requirement of reading a book and writing a report every week.

Becoming an honors student, Winfrey soon joined the drama club, student council and was chosen as one of two students in the state to go to the White House Conference on Youth.

"As strict as he was," Winfrey recalled, "my father had some concerns about me making the best of my life and would not accept anything less than what he thought was my best."

At age 19, she was hired by WVOL radio in Nashville and two years later, signed on with a TV station in Nashville as the youngest African-American reporter/anchor in the city's television history. During this time, she also attended Tennessee State University, where she majored in Speech Communications and Performing Arts.

"If you want to be successful, be excellent. If you want the best the world has to offer, offer the world your best," said the card taped to Oprah Winfrey's dormitory mirror.

Later, she moved to Chicago to host a morning show, *AM Chicago*, which became the number one local talk show in that market and when her ratings topped the venerated Phil Donahue – just one month after she began, the show was renamed *The Oprah Winfrey Show* and began national syndication.

In 1988, after establishing Harpo Studios, a production facility in Chicago, Winfrey became only the third woman in the American entertainment industry to own her own studio.

The Oprah Winfrey Show has remained the number one talk show for 19 consecutive seasons and is seen by an estimated 49 million viewers a week in the United States and is broadcast internationally in 122 countries.

After initiating the Oprah Book Club, every selection has become an instant bestseller.

When asked why she began the book club, her answer is as straightforward as her television persona, "My ability to read saved my life," she said. "I would have been an entirely different person had I not been taught to read when I was an early age. My entire life experience, my ability to believe in myself and even in my darkest moments, I knew there was another way. I knew there was a way out. I knew there was another kind of life because I had read about it. I knew there were other places and there was another way of being. It saved my life, so that's why I now focus my attention on trying to do the same thing for other people."

In 2000, Oprah's Angel Network began presenting a $100,000 "Use Your Life Award" to people who are using their lives to improve the lives of others. When *Forbes* magazine published its list of America's billionaires for the year 2003, it disclosed that Oprah Winfrey was the first African-American woman to become a billionaire.

Yet as she continues to be one of the most successful business people in the world, Winfrey still sees challenges ahead. "It's very difficult for me to even see myself as successful because I still see myself as in the process of becoming successful," she said to one interviewer. "To me, 'successful' is getting to the point where you are absolutely comfortable with yourself. And it does not matter how many things you have acquired."

In December 2003, Winfrey began a gift-giving pilgrimage to Africa. On her trip that year, she gave away 50,000 Christmas gifts to orphans and other desperately poor children. Inspired by the nuns who brought food and gifts to her house on Christmas when she was just 12 years old, and not satisfied with just playing Santa once a year, Winfrey eventually pledged to donate millions of dollars to build schools, empower women and help fight AIDS in Africa.

Winfrey is philosophical about her giveaways and her ability to help others. "Unless you choose to do great things with your success, it makes no different how much you are rewarded or how much power you have," she said. "But I also know that doing the best at this moment puts you in the best place for the next moment."

Winfrey is a living example of the seven defining moments – she is continually taking moments to commit, plan, act, connect, invest, change and conquer.

It doesn't matter who you are or where you come from. You can also create defining moments that have a powerful ripple effect in your own world.

So seize the moment. Create a defining moment for yourself or someone else today. You will be one step closer to leadership excellence!

• • • • •

"The spirit, the will to win, and the will to excel
are the things that endure. These qualities are so much
more important than the events that occur."
– Vince Lombardi, Football Coach

• • • • •

Reflecting on...

7 MOMENTS
... That Define Excellent Leaders

1 ... a Moment to COMMIT
Giving your all-time best

- **Think excellence**
  - You are the conductor of your own thoughts. No one else can control them for you.
  - Mentally reframe challenges to view them in a positive light.
  - True commitment never rests...keep pushing.
- **Create a compelling cause**
  - Answer the question, "*Why* do we do what we do?"
  - Keep it simple and easy to understand – people commit to what they can understand.
  - Think big – your cause should stir the emotions.
- **Secure your foundation**
  - Define and live by your team's foundational values.
  - Look at repeat problems for symptoms of cracks in your foundational values.
  - Define rules of engagement to reinforce your team values.

2 ... a Moment to PLAN
Taking time out

- **Set a high-definition vision**
  - Answer the four questions employees ask:
    1. What are we trying to achieve? (Goals)
    2. How are we going to achieve it? (Plans)
    3. How can I contribute? (Roles)
    4. What's in it for me? (Rewards)
  - Be more specific than you think you need to be.

○ Don't underestimate the intelligence of your employees.

● **Optimize your sweet spot**

    ○ Know your own leadership sweet spot by answering:

        1. What am I absolutely passionate about?

        2. Which tasks are very easy and natural for me to perform?

    ○ Match each employee's sweet spot to job requirements.

    ○ Redesign work to keep your team in their sweet spots.

● **Magnify your leadership**

    ○ Cut through the complexities of your operation and keep it simple.

    ○ Determine where the 80/20 Principle exists.

    ○ Leverage your vital few and minimize your trivial many.

3... a Moment to ACT
Making every minute count

● **Check your focus**

    ○ Your focus is a magnet for your life – look for excellence in all you do and excellence will find you.

    ○ Look at how you spend your time to check your focus.

    ○ Hard work is the best predictor of luck…and excellence.

● **Treasure your precious resources**

    ○ Say "No" to non-value-added activities.

    ○ Use your team's time, money and energy carefully, particularly in meetings.

    ○ Define what's "inside your boat" and stay focused on it.

● **Make real-time decisions**

    ○ Spend your time on the most important 20 percent of your decisions.

    ○ Collect the best information you can quickly, then use your leadership intuition to make the decision.

    ○ Listen at least 50 percent of the time.

4... a Moment to CONNECT
Reaching for the hands of time

● **Look beyond your employees**

   ○ Demonstrate an interest in your people, not just your employees.

   ○ Ensure at least 3 positive interactions to 1 negative interaction.

   ○ Go bananas with employee recognition – find ways to be creative and do it frequently.

● **Cultivate your network**

   ○ Methodically cultivate relationships – they are your lifeline.

   ○ Store information about your network in an easily accessible system.

   ○ Use your system of information and people to answer any question within 12 hours.

● **Ritualize your team**

   ○ Use rituals to reinforce your values.

   ○ Choose team rituals that fit your style.

   ○ Implement fewer rituals deeper.

5... a Moment to INVEST
Giving your time to improve a life

● **Inspire future leaders**

   ○ Mentor for success in work and life.

   ○ Coach well the first time to ensure learning and prevent re-coaching on the same skills.

   ○ Expose your team to a rich variety of experiences.

● **Live your legacy**

   ○ Focus on living your legacy instead of worrying about leaving it.

   ○ Give your life and wisdom away.

   ○ No investment is too small.

● **Exercise your brain**

   ○ Embrace lifelong learning.

   ○ Use your downtime as mental uptime – read, listen, learn, visualize.

   ○ Use mentors to get valuable answers to tough questions.

6... a Moment to CHANGE
Adapting to the times

● **Delight in discomfort**

  ○ Keep your momentum by seeking discomfort...and delighting in it!

  ○ When you feel like you are cruising to victory, take a look around...but not only at your opponents.

  ○ Lead beyond the status quo – always focus on the next level.

● **Know fear**

  ○ Get rational about your fears – identify the primary cause of your fear.

  ○ Get to know your fears and act on them – don't react to them.

  ○ Seek out different opinions before they come to you.

● **Multiply your power of one**

  ○ Convince yourself that YOU make the difference.

  ○ Change your world with one small act.

  ○ Make a positive change every day.

7... a Moment to CONQUER
Standing the test of time

● **Move through adversity**

  ○ Take inventory of what is lost and what is not lost.

  ○ Convert turning points into learning points.

  ○ Plan for the future but live in the present.

● **Take your stand**

  ○ Know your non-negotiables.

  ○ Rise courageously above the crowd.

  ○ Hang onto humility.

● **Stick to it**

  ○ Keep the faith in your leadership – stick to it long enough to win.

  ○ Ignore the odds and critics.

  ○ Never, ever give up!

More Ways
to Create Defining Moments
for Your Team

1. *7 Moments* **PowerPoint® Presentation**
   Introduce the *7 Moments* to your organization with this complete, cost-effective companion piece. All the main concepts and ideas in the book are reinforced in this professionally designed, downloadable presentation. It even includes speaking notes to make it a turnkey presentation for you! Use the presentation for kickoff meetings, training sessions, brown bag lunches or as a follow-up development tool. **$99.95**

2. **Keynote Presentation**
   Invite author Lee J. Colan to help your team accelerate their journey to leadership excellence. Lee's passion and enthusiasm create energizing and engaging presentations. He delivers practical, powerful tools participants can put to work right away. For more information, visit www.LeeColan.com.

3. *7 Moments* **Action Planner** These handy, three-panel action planners summarize the key points from the book and provide space for notes so participants can enhance their learning. Pk/20 **$49.95**

4. *7 Moments* **Quick Reference Desktop Tent**
   A defining and inspiring way to refer to and apply the key actions from the book!
   3½" x 6" Pk/20 **$59.95**

5. *7 Moments* **Learning Reinforcement Kit**
   Includes one each of: *7 Moments* book, action planner and a quick reference desktop tent. **$19.95**

6. *7 Moments* **Assessment**
   Take this free, online indicator based on the *7 Moments* book. A seven-minute investment yields a personalized plan to help you pursue leadership excellence! Visit www.LeeColan.com. Complimentary.

Recommended Reading
to Reinforce Each Moment...

1... a Moment to COMMIT

Orchestrating Attitude: Getting the Best from Yourself and Others

2... a Moment to PLAN

Sticking to It: The Art of Adherence

3... a Moment to ACT

Power Exchange: How to Boost Accountability and Performance in Today's Workforce

4... a Moment to CONNECT

Passionate Performance: Engaging Minds and Hearts to Conquer the Competition

5... a Moment to INVEST

Monday Morning Leadership: 8 Mentoring Sessions You Can't Afford to Miss

6... a Moment to CHANGE

The Next Level: Leading Beyond the Status Quo

7... a Moment to CONQUER

107 Ways to Stick to It: Practical Tips to Achieve the Success You Deserve

LEADERSHIP DEVELOPMENT PACKAGE
$199⁹⁵

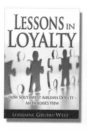
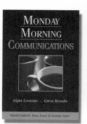

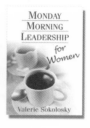

Visit www.**CornerStoneLeadership**.com
for additional books and resources.

Order Form

1-30 copies $14.95   31-100 copies $13.95   101+ copies $12.95

7 Moments ... That Define Excellent Leaders   _____ copies X _____   = $_____

7 Moments Companion Resources

PowerPoint® Presentation (downloadable)   _____ copies X $99.95   = $_____

Action Planners (Pk/20)   _____ pack(s) X $49.95   = $_____

Quick Reference Desktop Tent (Pk/20)   _____ pack(s) X $59.95   = $_____

7 Moments Learning Reinforcement Kit   _____ kit(s) X $19.95   = $_____
(Includes one each of *7 Moments*, Action
Planner, and Quick Reference Desktop Tent)

Additional Leadership Development Resources

Leadership Development Package   _____ pack(s) X $199.95   = $_____
(Includes all items shown on page 134)

Shipping & Handling $_____

Subtotal $_____

Sales Tax (8.25%-TX Only) $_____

Total (U.S. Dollars Only) $_____

Shipping and Handling Charges

Total $ Amount	Up to $50	$51-$99	$100-$249	$250-$1199	$1200-$2999	$3000+
Charge	$6	$9	$16	$30	$80	$125

Name _____ Job Title _____

Organization _____ Phone _____

Shipping Address _____ Fax _____

Billing Address _____ Email _____
(required when ordering PowerPoint® Presentation)

City _____ State _____ ZIP _____

❑ Please invoice (Orders over $200) Purchase Order Number (if applicable) _____

Charge Your Order: ❑ MasterCard   ❑ Visa   ❑ American Express

Credit Card Number _____ Exp. Date _____

Signature _____

❑ Check Enclosed (Payable to: CornerStone Leadership)

Mail
Phone 888.789.5323   **P.O. Box 764087**
Fax 972.274.2884   www.**CornerStoneLeadership**.com   **Dallas, TX 75376**

CornerStone◻
Leadership Institute